FOR A Sl
OF REWARD

A GLIMPSE AT THE LAW IN SCOTLAND

BY

ARCHIE BELL, QC

(Formerly Senior Sheriff of Glasgow and Strathkelvin)

MURDER : CULPABLE HOMICIDE : FRAUD :
EMBEZZLEMENT : BANK ROBBERY : ASSAULT : RAPE :
DIVORCE : INTERDICT : ROAD TRAFFIC :
COURT MARTIAL : GENERAL MEDICAL COUNCIL :
GENERAL DENTAL COUNCIL : PUBLIC INQUIRY :
CHILD CRIME : BURGH COURT : SMALL CLAIMS :
SCOTTISH LAND COURT
Plus GOLF & CRICKET.

A. A. BELL
1999

Published by A. A. BELL
20 Abercromby Place, Edinburgh EH3 6LB.

ISBN 0 9534771 0 X

Printed and bound by Lothian Print
7 New Lairdship Yards, Broomhouse Road, Edinburgh EH11 3UY

FOR A SHILLING
OF REWARD

CONTENTS

ABOUT THE AUTHOR

The author has had a wide interest and experience. As a schoolboy at The Leys School (long after James Hilton) he went to tea with "Mr Chips"; later rode a penny-farthing through a crowded Cambridge; uncovered a twenty-three year old female French spy in Madagascar; appeared in naval officer's uniform on stage in a Max Miller show at the Lewisham Hippodrome without reprimand (obeying a senior officer); was offered professional terms to play a full Shakespeare season in the Byre Theatre, St Andrews—Bassanio in the Merchant of Venice and Benedick in Much Ado About Nothing; stood for Parliament; was President of St Andrews University R.F.C. (a founder member of the Scottish Rugby Union) and represented the University at rugby football, hockey, cricket and association football; served also on the governing body of Scotland's oldest university; as a director of Heart of Midlothian F.C. drafted the original plan still in operation for a ten-club Premier League; was President of the Grange Cricket Club and President of the Scottish Cricket Union; named, and was President of the Capercailzies a Scottish cricket side which toured Hong Kong twice, Malaysia, Barbados and Western Canada; fired the noon-day gun in Hong Kong; worked otherwise for Her Majesty's Government; and defended men when the price of his failure might have meant the gallows for them. Such pleasures he has now sacrificed for a quiet seat in the Big Room of the Royal and Ancient or relaxation with his M.C.C. friends in front of the Pavilion at Lord's.

FOREWORD

This book, largely anecdotal, and paradoxically without deference to legal discipline, is compiled from random recollections of forty eight years in the law (1947–1995) without recourse to record or research. It follows no chronological pattern.

An attempt has been made to display for the ordinary reader different facets of the legal diamond, a range of human reactions, from fear to flippancy, and delight to despair, which pervade them, and a few of the characters involved. Some names have been altered and some omitted so that those involved should be exposed to humour but not to hurt.

The illustrations from the Bar (1949–1973) precede the enormous increase in work now available for Counsel, the rush of new prospectors good, bad and indifferent to stake out their claim, and the soaring financial rewards even to some who, a generation before, would have found it almost impossible to eke out a living. A reminder that the reward for professional skills is based less on expertise and more on what the current market will bear.

The present market may well have peaked but will never drop to previous levels.

These years before the so-called fat cats lapped from the bowl of cream are also mercifully a far cry from the days in the nineteenth century when the young advocate, Robert Louis Stevenson, describing Parliament House was moved to write:—

"Intelligent men have been walking here daily for ten or twenty years without a rag of business or a shilling of reward. In process of time they may perhaps be made the Sheriff-Substitute and fountain of justice at Lerwick or Tobermory".

The writer, the fifth successive generation of his family to practise law, escaped starvation, Lerwick and Tobermory and, despite in the mid-sixties having the largest 'silk practice' in Scotland in both crime and divorce, much more than a rag of business, was happy to follow the Scottish legal tradition "for a shilling of reward".

1.

PROTECTING A LADY

One of my early sallies into advocacy took place in the old Edinburgh Burgh Court where lay Magistrates could apply their minds to delivering verdicts, unfettered by any legal training. The old jokes abounded of alleged observations from the bench to the accused:—

"You wouldn't be here if you hadn't done something."

"Not guilty, but don't do it again."

The City Prosecutor was James Heatly. The most distinctive feature of his office—by that I do not mean his occupation but his head-quarters—was a wooden statuette of the idolised Hearts centre forward of the fifties, Willie Bauld. This distinction he shared with a well known Edinburgh hostelry, that of Paddy Crossan another Hearts stalwart who retired in 1933. Later strangely his son, Pat Crossan who flirted with a legal training ran a pleasant New Town hostelry called "The Tilted Wig" much patronised by the legal fraternity.

The case which took me to the Burgh Court, however, was not concerned with Willie Bauld or Paddy Crossan but with another whose name had become prominent in a different game. I had been instructed to defend Ava who had earned a reputation as Edinburgh's leading lady of the streets. I have no doubt that it was earned at great personal sacrifice and considerable cost in shoe leather.

At that time in the early fifties prostitution in the streets, even in the New Town of Edinburgh, was still rife. Queen Street was a favourite perambulating area for the girls who regarded themselves as a cut above their Rose Street sisters, and it was here that the cruising Casanovas stopped their vehicles in order to invite the ladies to take the weight off their legs.

Not all women walking in Queen Street of an evening, however, were bent on increasing their income by granting temporary tenancy of a part of their anatomy. It was even bandied about—truthfully, I think—that myopic drivers from time to time had been known to make propositions to the innocent ladies, at least so far as street-walking was concerned, of the wives of members of the Faculty of Advocates on their way to their gracious homes in Heriot Row or Moray Place.

In fact at one stage it became so embarrassing to some that, after complaints a trap was laid by putting plain clothes policewomen on Queen Street at intervals to snare the amorous motorists. Of an evening three were brought in. This I had on good authority.

One was a company representative, one was a civil servant and one was a Church of Scotland Minister. They were simply given a warning.

Amongst all these courtesans, however, Ava was queen. Whether Mr. W.S. Trench, Solicitor, or my clerk thought that this young counsel looked hungry, or the Dean of the Faculty of Advocates felt unavailable, I was picked on as the man to defend her.

The sniggers and schoolboyish innuendoes from some of my young bar contemporaries I was able to withstand. "Why did she pick on you Archie?" said one with a knowing leer.

I eyed him frostily.

"The reason I was instructed to defend her professionally". I replied stuffily, "is because I am one of the few people at the bar who does not know her socially". It was, even if wide of the mark, a fair enough answer.

On this occasion Ava had not been charged with plying her usual trade. The charge, one of assault, did, however arise indirectly from this.

She had formed an attachment with a well-know Parliament House solicitor who had previously been a Procurator-Fiscal in Glasgow but who had decided to set up his own private solicitor's business in Edinburgh. The same gentleman later scarpered to Dublin, and then to Canada, but that is another story, and did not concern Ava.

At the time in question Ava and Jackie were having what is now popularly known as a relationship, it was suggested, to mutual advantage. While he attended to her business affairs she in return paid by providing her own professional services for him.

A reasonable arrangement you may think.

Unfortunately one evening when Jackie had not returned home to his better half, and "had stayed late at the office" to be joined by Ava, a row developed between the two.

Ava was angry.

While Jackie was in a state of undress Ava took the trouble to telephone her client's wife to tell her exactly where she was and, as if further proof were required, to inform her that Jackie had a mole on his right thigh. She was not referring to any family pet, and as Jackie was not a zoologist Jackie's wife was doubtless aware of the significance. Following this incident, perhaps on his wife's advice, Jackie sought to cool the relationship.

But women are a bit like flypapers. If you touch them it can be a ghastly job getting rid of them. Ava was no exception. She proceeded to harry the wretched Jackie and eventually took, according to him, to assaulting him in public. The matter was reported to the police.

Thus Ava found herself in the Burgh Court entrusted to my tender professional inexperience.

Evidence was led. Jackie himself spoke to a vigorous assault in which blows, dare I say, were rained on him with an umbrella.

For some reason, however, the supporting Crown witness who was to supply corroboration of the assault had not appeared. The City Prosecutor naturally asked for an adjournment so that the witness could be brought at a later date.

I was quick to chance my fledgling arm.

Jumping to my feet I declared to a rather shaken and frightened female Bailie, who felt inclined to back away from this bewigged young lion, that it was monstrous that my client who had already suffered strain from having been brought to Court should be subjected to the additional anxiety of having to appear again after an interval with this serious charge still hanging over her head. (This was a lot of codswallop, for whether this particular Bailie knew it or not, Ava was no stranger to the Court).

I demanded, yes "demanded" (brave boy) that the charge against her should be dismissed and my client found Not Guilty.

The Bailie quivered and hesitated. "Case dismissed" she said.

Here indeed was an early forensic triumph.

Strangely Ava's immediate reaction was not one of unqualified approval. She had expected to go into the witness box. She had dressed for the occasion and, like most women, she had wanted to have her say.

Women are not happy if they are not allowed to have their say.

However, Ava soon cooled down and expressed her gratitude, and I was shortly to receive from Mr. Trench—through my clerk—the handsome fee of £10 for my trouble. At this end of the market not even guineas. How long it took her to earn it, I do not know. According to her solicitor she made a steady income. This was supplemented, he said, by occasional bonuses accruing from rugby internationals at Murrayfield, the General Assembly of the Church of Scotland in May and the odd visit of a foreign battleship to the Forth. This I add not as a coarse embellishment but as what Mr. Trench insisted was a matter of fact. Put in perspective of course he was talking of small minorities. Clearly even Ava could not have coped with a 60,000 Murrayfield crowd.

It is interesting that, as with those in other fields of conduct struck at by the law, Ava had her own "code". Many a time thereafter in late afternoon while returning home from Parliament House to the New Town I would see her standing patiently in a doorway like a piece of psychedelic bait waiting for a fish to rise. Her shock of artificially coloured hair, her over painted face and her lurid purple tight fitting ensemble could hardly be missed.

For all the occasions I walked past her in professional dress, plainly recognised by her, whether I was alone or with a colleague, she never once by twitch of her mouth, or even the flicker of an eyelid, showed the slightest sign of recognition. She was a true professional.

She did not wish to embarrass me.

Unfortunately, quite involuntarily I imagine, she did not keep her one hundred per cent record.

One evening, on the way to the old juridical library up in Charlotte Square, so faithfully and regularly patronised at that time by such eager young accumulators of legal knowledge as Ivor Guild WS later a veritable pillar of Charlotte Square, and my ex fellow office apprentice in Messrs. McGrigor, Donald & Co. Solicitors, Professor David Walker QC, and looked after by dear old Mrs Windybank, I jumped quickly on to a tram car and sat hurriedly down beside a middle aged lady on one of the seats at the back which faced inwards.

I suddenly caught the eye of the only occupant of the other side sitting directly opposite. With instinctive recognition of a known face she smiled. It was Ava in full battledress.

Oh dear! The woman next to me stiffened, gave me a nasty look, and moved farther away from me.

I do not know what became of poor Ava.

2.

THE DAY THE KING DIED

It was the sixth of February 1952.

The First Division of the Court of Session in Edinburgh the highest Court of civil jurisdiction in Scotland, was assembled for another day's business. Lord President Cooper, Lord Carmont and Lord Russell were there, but the fourth member Lord Keith (later in the House of Lords, Lord Keith of Avonholm) was missing.

To them it must have been a hum-drum affair. Déja-vu. A dull, dreary appeal from the Sheriff Court across in the Lawnmarket, about fish-boxes, in which it had been suggested that the Sheriff had given the wrong decision. Only a young junior counsel on either side.

No "silks" of substance on which Scotland's premier judges could whet their judicial appetite.

Really, although no one would have said so outwardly, the whole case, as well as the fish-boxes, stank.

Lord Cooper whose high complexion always appeared to have been purchased at great expense (which it had not) was smallish of stature but firm of jaw. He always read his papers carefully beforehand and had probably decided already how it should go. This was the criticism made by losers before him, never by winners, that he had already made up his mind. He might have spent a happier day no doubt on one of his many extraneous activities—no longer as Lord Advocate discussing with Tom Johnston the Secretary of State for Scotland, the country to which he was devoted, or driving his Rolls-Royce, or shopping for his dear elderly mother, or examining with a critical eye the heating system in Parliament House just to see that everything was in working order.

With his infinite knowledge it was the regret of many, however, even later, that he never turned to writing. "Well", he would say crisply to more experienced Counsel with a tug of the gown that was slipping on his right shoulder, "That's your first point, what is your second?" This was a polite way of telling the pleader that he was getting nowhere with his current argument and had better try a new tack. A precise and formidable judge whose *ex tempore* judgements were a model, he maintained his clarity of utterance to the very end.

At a BBC meeting he is said to have declared with lucid precision "I think that I am going to be ill", his last coherent utterance. He promptly had a cerebral haemorrhage from which he never recovered.

Lord Carmont's high pitched voice and sharp humour were at their best in the morning. In the afternoon, being older, he would close his eyes. Woe betide the Counsel who assumed that he had gone to sleep. Suddenly his eyes would open and, with it, his mouth, to put a telling question. I remember once, later, being the victim of his penetrating enquiry. I was slightly put aback and gave a highly non-committal answer. "Ah" he said teasingly. "Mr Bell you just want to see how the judicial cattle are going to jump". "I agree my Lord" I replied, "but with respect I would not have put it quite like that". He gave a chuckle, his eyes closed again, and we continued.

It was Lord Carmont whose firm Roman Catholic discipline was later brought to the rising tide of violent crime in Glasgow to such a punitive degree that in the underworld they talked of a heavy sentence as "buying a Carmont". Some colleagues began to emulate him and when Lord Keith delivered a ten year sentence, in a case in which about three years had been expected, a thunder-struck supporter broke the hushed silence in the public gallery by exclaiming in basic Glaswegian "Oh fur f—'s sake". He was quickly hustled away.

Lord Russell was a benign and kindly, soft spoken, man with a distinguished head of white hair. His son Muir Russell, CBE, slightly junior to me at the Bar gave many years sterling service as a Sheriff in Aberdeen. Lord Russell might have been happier in his beautiful garden at Barnton or playing golf at Bruntsfield or Muirfield.

It was at Bruntsfield, a golf club from which I resigned membership in 1955 a week before I was asked to join the Council there, that I saw his patience tested. Lord Mackintosh and I were playing against him and a new member of the Bar named McNab Chassels, a speedy rugby footballer of the same Glasgow High School FP side as Wilson Shaw who captained Scotland's Triple Crown winning side of 1938. Chassels was less quick in his assimilation of Gloag and Henderson's introduction to the Law of Scotland. It was the third round of the Bench and Bar foursomes. The first two rounds were always played at Muirfield, later rounds at any agreed venue. We were winning for the simple reason that every time Chassels played his Lordship's ball it landed unerringly in a bunker where his elderly partner had to descend gingerly to dig it out.

Eventually Lord Russell who was becoming a little tired of trench warfare, or should it be desert warfare, chided him gently. Chassels an engaging fellow was not one for tact or reticence. "Well Sir", he said in his breezy Cambuslang fashion, no doubt mistakenly imagining that he was paying a compliment, "You play out of them so well I thought that I might learn something". He might well have learned the value of knowing when to keep one's mouth shut; Lord Russell did not reply. A kindness on his part.

Not surprisingly, Chassels was soon called to another bar, this one a public house in Hamilton which he purchased. There, direct pleading would be more readily appreciated and the rewards greater than he might have expected from a career in Parliament House.

Perhaps our three judges would have been happier if it had been "February week". This was a traditional break for a whole week in the middle of the Candlemas Term when the Court of Session did not sit. Lofty seniors would sigh with relief and say that it gave them a chance to catch up with their written work. Others, less busy, would affect to do so in order to foster the impression that they also were bowed down with work. For some hungry young juniors however it was simply another week's opportunity lost to earn an honest crust; or even, would you believe it, to be in Court "gaining experience" without even a crust. It was Lord Cooper who finally abolished this anachronism.

Back to the Sixth of February 1952. I had been two years two months at the Bar, a novice to be addressing the man (Lord Cooper) who had sought to find a relationship between myself and George Joseph Bell, one of Scotland's leading jurists, my opponent Harry Keith had been at the Bar some three months less. It was his father Lord Keith who was missing. Whether he thought the idea of his son pleading before him unbearable I do not know.

My only previous experience of father Keith had been on a curling rink at Haymarket where some members of the Bench and Bar enjoyed membership of the Coates Curling Club. This was a very old club which had had its origins or rather its expression on a frozen pond in the corner of the Grange Cricket Club ground at Raeburn Place, Edinburgh, a club of which I was later fortunate enough to be President for five years. I do not know if Sheriff David Smith of Kilmarnock whose researches produced the History of Scottish Curling will be aware of this.

The part of the ground where curling took place had, however, been sold off by the Grange-Academical Trust to make way for the Tanfield Bowling Club which provided recreational facilities for workers who produced at Tanfield the *Scottish Daily Mail* on a site now occupied by the Standard Life Assurance Company. An early indication of our move towards a classless society.

I was in a sense glad that Lord Keith was not present to hear my argument. His Lordship could be less than over-joyed if you put a curling stone where it should not have been, or alternatively if you did not put it where it should have been. I could not have guaranteed to address him with an argument in which everything would slide into its proper place.

Harry Keith was on his feet delivering very ably; Now of course, the august and distinguished Lord Keith of Kinkell he delivered for years leading judgements in the House of Lords.

As he spoke he was suddenly interrupted by a Court officer who rushed in and whispered something in Lord Cooper's ear. His Lordship sat up sharply. I could not guess what the official had said, but it was obviously of some importance. Was the building on fire? No. Had Hearts won the Scottish Cup? No, not on a February morning. The Court Officer I should interject, was a rabid Hearts supporter who gave them up in disgust when the club sold Dave McKay to Tottenham Hotspur for about £28,000.

Turning suddenly to Lord Carmont on his right I heard Lord Cooper say distinctly and dramatically in an audible whisper: "The King. He's dead" Four or five words. With a motion, and without being informed, we were bidden to carry on. Harry Keith who was on his feet continued. Minutes later the case was over.

Lord Cooper adjourned the Court.

Shortly afterwards he convened the entire Bench of the Court of Session in the First Division Court room. Judges, Counsel, solicitors, clerks the press and the public crowded in.

To a hushed audience he announced that news had been received of the death that morning at Sandringham of His Majesty, King George VI. As a mark of respect all courts would be adjourned for the remainder of that day.

Everyone trooped out.

Only in Counsel's robing room was there a flap of activity. Court mourning decreed that all King's Counsel, who automatically became Queen's Counsel, would require to wear "weepers". These were white bands of cloth sewn on to the sleeves of their coats on which they might wipe away their tears of grief for the departed monarch.

It was the sixth of February 1952. The King was dead. Now as I write all the judges who assembled that day are dead, and as Lord Cooper was wont to say movingly in paying tribute when a colleague died. "will only be remembered in his judgements"'

I respectfully beg to disagree. I recall with affection in this recollection of a day of death the help and courtesy they all showed to young Counsel.

I should like to think that for the better administration of a proud legal system in Scotland that that tradition will survive even longer than many of their judgements even if the thirteen judges are increased to one hundred and thirteen.

3.

FOWL PLAY

A large sum of money—in notes—the proceeds of a bank robbery, was hidden by the thief while the heat was on.

In his wisdom he chose to bury his loot in a hen-run, no doubt being satisfied that the inhabitants would not squawk on him.

Perhaps he thought also that at some future day he would be able to scratch a living. At any rate he was cock-a-hoop at that stage.

Unfortunately somebody gave the game away. The money was dug up and he was apprehended.

At his trial in the High Court in Glasgow it was put to him forcibly that he was the person who had hidden this money in the hen-run.

The accused, although not chicken, was reluctant to answer. Perhaps he did not wish to crow about it. Although naturally egged on by counsel he withdrew into his shell as one might put it. When pressed further instead of seeking refuge in a flat denial, he remained totally silent on his perch.

Irritated, Counsel asked one further question, "Did you think" he shouted "that it was just chicken feed?"

4.

ON THE WAY TO THE WOOLSACK

Lord Blades sat on the Bench biting his finger-nails.

This characteristic gnawing exercise was not to supplement a meagre intake of porridge at breakfast, but was a signal that he was uncertain how to resolve the legal argument before him.

Some Judges, curiously, do display uncertainty at times which, to the careful observer, may show for example in their facial or neck muscles, or may more plainly be detected in their irritability.

"Danny" Blades was not an irritable man. A son of the manse from Duns in Berwickshire he could easily have been mistaken in the street for a cleric with his black hat, spectacles, furled umbrella and walking, when it was not raining, with his raincoat draped characteristically over his left shoulder. I liked him, not only because his pleasant daughter, sadly now dead, was kind enough occasionally to look after my small children. He had not been born great, or acquired greatness but had really had it thrust upon him. This was a challenge he was prepared to accept.

Although not a socialist he was one of the early recipients of the post-war Labour benefice. While in the distant past there had been plenty of Whigs and Tories at the Scottish Bar, and later an abundance of Liberals (of whom he was one) and Tories in fairly equal number, whose ranks could supply a new judge, generally depending on which political party was in power, it was not easy for the Labour Government of 1945 despite their large majority in the House of Commons.

There were then, unlike now, few genuine socialists amongst members of the Faculty of Advocates who tended in the main still to be drawn from a restricted social background. Rather than promote a Tory it was felt desirable if possible to appoint Liberals such as Lord Blades and Lord Guthrie (who was only about eighteen months a KC when he was elevated to the Court of Session Bench) along of course with any others politically inactive and thus undeclared previously who, in furtherance of their careers, had acquired a sudden taste for egalitarianism.

Danny had first been Solicitor-General. At the Bar he had not always expressed himself to best advantage. Appearing in a rape case appeal for example, he had drawn the attention of the Bench to a matter which he thought significant, "As Your Lordships well know" he declared authoritatively "if you rape a woman on the grass you may have green stains on your trousers". The indignant disclaimer came swiftly from Lord Moncrieff "Mr Blades, I do **not** know".

Now Danny was gnawing his finger-nails and clearly having difficulty. A judge of course must make up his mind. That is what he was then paid the princely sum of £5000 a year to do. Some Judges it is said see the argument from both sides so clearly that they cannot decide who is right or wrong. Others at times find the wood and the trees indistinguishable. Rather than sit on the fence they must come down on one side even if it is the wrong one. After all, there must be something to occupy an appeal Court who can point out loftily with twenty twenty hindsight where the original Judge or Sheriff has erred.

The case was one of little moment except to the pursuer. A reparation action in which an injured workman was suing his employer for damages arising out of their negligence. Such cases were ten-a-penny.

In the fifties solid powerful trade unions backed their members with financial muscle. Dogged insurance companies resisted these claims on behalf of the employers. The emphasis in Scotland on lengthy formalised pleadings, setting out what was in issue between the parties, gave the eager academic lawyer the opportunity in debate to hack, niggle at or stick pins in his opponents' case. This of course was at a preliminary stage with not a witness or a party in sight.

The subtle defenders' advocate sought to show that, even if the pursuer were to prove everything he set out to prove, it would be insufficient in law to entitle him to succeed. The case should be thrown out without hearing evidence. The pursuer's counsel would agree that, even if some of his averments were of doubtful relevancy, there was sufficient at least to entitle him to go to proof, even if he did not obtain the odds-on favourite for ultimate success of a jury trial.

Such was the argument in this case and such was Lord Blades' dilemma.

When I read the pleadings in the pursuer's case, not drafted by myself as I recollect, they appeared adequate to me to entitle the pursuer to the proof which he sought, not, as I anticipated then, the reasonably sound investment of a jury trial. There were legal difficulties inappropriate for a jury to resolve.

The defenders' counsel clearly did not agree. I had not appeared against him before. He was a "new boy" and was virtually cutting his teeth. No one had talked of encountering him in court, but he was said to be, academically, a bright chap.

His name was James Peter Hymers Mackay.

It soon became clear that he was devoted to this early brief. He handled its words with loving and intimate care and, if offered a bet, which would not have been welcome to this devout member of the Free Church of Scotland, he could probably have recited it backwards. This of course would only have confused poor Lord Blades further. He was still not certain how to deal with it reading forwards.

Mackay's grasp of the written pleadings and of the legal questions was immaculate, but his quiet, shy and rather hesitant court presentation fell well short of the same standard. In this his inexperience showed. Despite my argument in reply that this was clearly a case which merited a proof, Lord Blades, to my surprise and to my vague annoyance, jumped in the other direction and dismissed the action.

Full marks to James Peter Hymers Mackay.

Had I been a football manager I would have offered him terms to sign on immediately as a promising junior. All I did, however, was to tell some others about him. I happened just afterward to meet George Emslie, then still a junior (later Lord President and Lord Justice General) outside of the court room and walked up and down Parliament Hall telling him at length about the abilities of our new fellow junior. George listened intently, asked a number of pertinent questions, and it was not long before some others in higher places were taking this potential "star" under their wing in order to help him.

Real ability, in my experience, was always respected and welcomed without jealousy in Parliament House. I hope that it still is to-day.

As to the case itself, Lord Blades had been wrong to dismiss it, and his decision was reversed on appeal. That was no discredit to Mackay.

Little did I dream that the diffident young man at my side, the son of a railway signal man and, surprisingly, the first George Heriot's School man to be called to the Scottish Bar had just put his foot on the first rung of the ladder to begin a long steady upward climb which would take him eventually to two illustrious offices, Lord Advocate and then, despite his Scottish background, through the good graces of Mrs Thatcher to the highest legal office, that of Lord Chancellor.

5.

THROUGH A GLASS LIGHTLY

Four of us had been briefed by Laurence Dowdall, Glasgow's leading criminal practitioner at the time, to appear in Glasgow High Court to defend two CID officers on a serious charge of fraud.

Lionel Daiches QC, Ewan Stewart (later Lord Stewart), myself, and a comparative newcomer to the Bar, Sir Ian Moncreiffe of that Ilk, whose knowledge of crime had been gleaned more fully from the history of the Scottish aristocracy to which be belonged than to a first-hand experience of the contemporary Scottish underworld to which he did not.

As we sat together at the broad table in the North Court in front of the Clerk, with the Judge looming high in front of us, and the public and potential jurors sitting silent in the benches behind, up-to-date thoughts on the case raced through our minds.

At the sign of any sudden brainwave from one we all craned forward and huddled together to listen intently.

Sir Ian, as a newcomer to the Bar, was not inhibited by his inexperience and was full of startling ideas.

Not all of these could be dismissed, for behind his Sir Percy Blakeney façade, there lurked a considerable intelligence. In 1946 after the war for example when the Scots Guards wondered what to do with him, as no doubt did others, Ian said to someone in the War Office, as he described to me, blinking as usual, "Well, I've never been to Russia". They promptly sent him to the Embassy in Moscow. Later, apart from his deep knowledge of heraldry, his expositions on economic sabotage in Europe were fascinating.

On this occasion, however, he did himself less than justice. As we strained forward to listen to his inspired thought, he motioned to the huge glass bowl in front of the Clerk which contained the numbers and names of those from whom with fitting solemnity the jury was about to be balloted.

"Do you know what I'd like to do?" he said, pointing a delicate finger at the large transparent container,

"I'd like to pee in that".

That wish like many of Ian's, particularly the cupidinous one said to have been directed much later to Mrs Thatcher, remained unfulfilled.

6.

EVERYBODY HAPPY

Danny was a bookmaker: a big man of sallow complexion and black hair, dressed predictably in a bright Glen Urquhart check. He exuded a likeable but nervous warmth of presence which could chill instantly to a fierce bluntness, like the sun vanishing swiftly behind a dark cloud.

Whether by instinct, habit or stress, or to escape from haunting memories he had come, on occasion, to drink fiercely and, since judgement is an early victim of alcohol, to have little regard for the consequences.

Like most of his breed he revelled in material comfort and, like most, possessed in ample measure, the eloquent token to achieve it—folding money.

He had perhaps more reason than most to savour it all.

Years of internment in a Japanese prisoner of war camp had ravaged him physically and mentally. Despite a dogged recovery these legacies were still with him. His face was deeply lined. Inwardly the hidden scars on his mind had one which would never heal: an abiding obsession about captivity.

Danny hated prisons.

With a cruel and forgetful irony, however, fate had reached out into his post-war rehabilitation. Driving his car one night he was involved in a horrific accident which resulted in the death of an innocent person. Danny, no stranger to death, or to the pain and suffering which he was now accused of causing, found himself up on a charge of culpable homicide.

The charge was serious enough to cause worry to anyone, but it was the possible consequences which struck him forcibly —imprisonment.

John Cameron QC (later the First Lord Cameron) who was in his time Dean of the Faculty of Advocates, was briefed to defend him.

Despite the skill and experience of such eminent Counsel, there was only one outcome.

Danny was sentenced to a period of eighteen months' imprisonment.

The sentence was served without incident and, in the years that followed, he again became acclimatised to comfort and to freedom. One of these freedoms was to drive a powerful motor car.

One might have thought that he would have approached drink with more caution, and driving with equal care: that he might never be accused of combining the two.

It is interesting to reflect that in the fifties, however, there were still happily far fewer cars to choke up the roads, drivers in general showed more consideration, and it was not an offence to drive a car having taken drink *per se*. The public use or abuse of the habit of "one for the road" was not only practised on a large scale but, unless resulting in actual danger to others, viewed by a large number of the population with an amazing degree of tolerance.

There were no breathalysers to provide the modern clear cut "verdict". To drive after drinking was only struck at by the law if the driver was "driving while under the influence of drink (or drugs) to such an extent as to be incapable of having proper control of a motor vehicle". We were still with the Road Traffic Act 1930.

Danny found himself on such a charge, the notorious "Section Fifteen".

Conviction would have little effect on his business: the punter is not concerned with the private life of the bookmaker whom he subsidises so freely and in such generous measure. A fine could be met with a wallet and the shrug of a shoulder.

Prison was a different matter and it preyed on Danny's mind.

His solicitors contacted Freddie Main WS who rang my clerk and I was briefed to appear for him in Dumfries Sheriff Court at a fee of sixty guineas which was considered reasonably generous for an experienced senior junior Counsel in those days.

I mention it not because today a raw junior may on occasion be paid much more for attending as a spectator and taking a few notes, but only because it has a later relevance.

I had a consultation with Danny in Edinburgh and then, on the day before his trial, made my way to the delightful town where it would take place, Dumfries, having booked into the comfortable hotel which I usually patronised when in that part of the country.

In the morning I met his local solicitor and then Danny as well. We discussed the final details of the case. He was clearly agitated. He obviously wanted to speak to me alone.

Chance came. The solicitor was called away.

In a trice he came to the point. He took out his wallet. "Mr Bell, I don't want to go to jail. There's a thousand pounds here for you if I don't go to jail". This was certainly an advance on his solicitor's sixty guineas.

I smiled gently and said that I would do my best. He put his wallet and the greenbacks away, and just afterwards his local solicitor returned.

The trial proceeded—the details do not matter—but at the end of the day, all was well. No question of Danny going to prison. His gratitude was genuine. As you may imagine as a man of his word he wanted to see me alone.

Again chance came, and his solicitor left us.

Whipping out his wallet he waved a thousand pounds in cash in front of me. "Mr Bell, can I settle with you now?" His gratitude and his wish to settle were both genuine.

Having assured him that his solicitor would get a fee note from my clerk at a later stage he relaxed and departed quite happily. I was indeed later paid the princely sum of sixty guineas.

Many months passed.

Then, one day I was instructed, as often, by Dan McKay SSC a well known Edinburgh solicitor, to appear for a client of his in the same Sheriff Court and, following my usual custom, I arrived the night before the case in the same local hotel in Dumfries.

I went into the bar before dinner. There was only one other person there. He was standing alone and hailed me immediately. At the end of the long arm of coincidence a welcoming hand was held out to shake mine. Yes, Danny's

We chatted on general topics until suddenly the mood changed and he became confidential.

"You know Mr Bell, I was amazed at how little your fee was in that case you took for me". I thought back—yes sixty guineas —but said nothing.

"You see," he went on looking round to see that no one was listening (I can never understand why people do this. I have yet to encounter a barman who is bound by the official Secrets Act or is a Trappist monk or a deaf mute). "I received a bill from my solicitors". He mentioned a figure many many times in excess of my own fee.

It is seldom in my experience that Counsel will meet a former client, and if it happens it is not to discuss fees.

Danny continued. "I said to them, Mr Bell did all the work. You only took some statements. How can you charge so much?"

An explanation was given which Danny found to be totally unsatisfactory.

"You know what I did" he said pausing to see if I was paying attention. "I took out my wallet (This had the ring of truth). I laid X pounds—the figure mentioned—on the table in cash" I was listening.

The solicitor scooped it up smartly and said "Thank you". The matter was thus concluded to the satisfaction of both.

I, too, I suppose, was quite happy. In those days cases did not fall off a conveyor belt. It was only success in court which brought further fruitful briefs to Counsel and not as now, simply the enormous increase in law-breaking and the availability of Legal Aid which guarantees employment and payment irrespective of the standard of performance, or even the degree of application.

7.

ONE OF OURS

Arthur Duffes KC (then QC) was endowed with a kindliness and an old-fashioned courtesy. I first met him in his later years. He would emerge from his large house in Abercromby Place, the sort of place over the divided carcass of which accountants and property developers have been wont to haggle recently, stick in hand and wearing a tall wide brimmed hat. He would pause in the street to speak with a benign inclination of the head much affected by ministers and friendly schoolmasters. His sister in fact was owner and headmistress of St Serf's Girls School at the other end of Abercromby Place (now chopped into "luxurious and prestigious" new town flats) under which the planners in their wisdom have allowed the benefit of a Chinese restaurant.

One would not readily have surmised that in his earlier days Arthur had been a bit of a rebel, had tackled some of the legal establishment fiercely, and had been a redoubtable champion of many of modest means who could ill have afforded to raise an action against their employers in the old days of Workmen's Compensation cases when there was no Legal Aid available, and where often in actions described as "speculative" Counsel's only hope of a fee depended on winning and recovering expenses from the other side.

No win, no fee. Whether through missionary work by two successive Scottish Lord Chancellors, or otherwise, mirabile dictu England has now adopted this "novel" and revolutionary procedure with which one was familiar with in practice in Scotland over forty years ago but which of course has largely been eroded by the introduction of Legal Aid.

Duffess' career as with many "rebels" never brought him

high office, and at last he settled down to be a National Insurance Commissioner. Not exciting.

The challenge of the courts, however, still beckoned to Arthur and, forgetting the old adage of retired boxers that "they never come back", he decided, late in life, to return to the fray.

He had not so far been in action since his return when my clerk, Gilbert McWhannell, broke the news to me. "So-and-so QC is out of that case next week and you'll be with Mr Duffes".

We proceeded to do battle as Arthur had done many more times than I, for an injured workman who was suing his employers for injury arising out of their negligence.

The old man with, I confess, a bit of prompting at times from myself, was making the most of rather flimsy material.

Counsel not otherwise engaged were prepared to take such cases for nothing even if the odds and the cases were long.

Financial greed was not then the main characteristic of a Scottish advocate although certain solicitors would have found it difficult to avoid the charge. In one such case I appeared for a man who told the jury about sustaining three broken ribs in a tramcar accident. It did not need the skill of defenders' counsel, Jack Mackenzie-Stuart Q.C. (later Lord Mackenzie-Stuart the first British judge in Europe and Chairman of the European Court) to convince the jury that the three ribs had been broken earlier in another accident which had been the source of a successful earlier claim but had not been re-broken as claimed in the tramcar. No win, no fee. Arthur Duffes no doubt had many such experiences but his optimism bubbled.

Eventually with a ring of artificial confidence which existed long before the advertisements for toothpaste he announced that, with documents, he was closing the pursuer's case.

The defenders led their first witness and the old man proceeded to cross-examine. He was warming to the conflict and his enthusiasm for the cause increased with every question he asked.

Age can be cruel, however, and sometimes it plays tricks on the mind.

The defenders led their second witness, and again my senior cross-examined with gusto. He seemed pleased with his work-out.

Before sitting down he announced to an astonished Lord Strachan that, with documents, he was closing the pursuer's case.

Tugging his gown gently I whispered in his ear "We've closed our case. That is THEIR second witness".

He reacted instantly as a true professional. Leaping to his feet he answered:—

"I apologise, my Lord, that witness was so much in our favour that I thought he was one of our own".

Lord Strachan who was wont to sit impassively, listening intently, sometimes with a hand cupped over his ear, to every argument, good or bad, without change in expression, permitted himself the slightest movement of the extreme ends of his lips.

8.

CARRY ON DRIVER

Sheriff Dobie who sat in Glasgow Sheriff Court was a kindly balding man and an able lawyer. The two do not necessarily go together. It was the exception rather than the rule when I appeared in front of him as a young counsel to find a solicitor on the shrieval bench, and certainly to find one who commanded such respect. He was the author of several text books in his day about the Sheriff Court not to mention in lighter vein 'Plain Tales from the Courts'. They were widely read and accepted beyond the confines of Campbeltown in Argyll from which he had moved to Glasgow. Six or seven Sheriffs were then able to operate Glasgow Sheriff Court as opposed to over twenty at the present time.

I still remember Sheriff Dobie with respect and affection.

My first appearance in front of him was—as became a habit for me in the fifties around the country—to defend on "drunk driving". This was a profitable way for young counsel to spend a Monday when the Court of Session did not sit. While the expression "travelling junior" was used by the wives of some of the members of the bar who had achieved eminence to distinguish and underline those of lesser rank than their husbands, I was happy to take to the road than rather be a member of the junior bar—of whom there were many in those days—who did not get even that opportunity.

There was nothing demeaning or inconvenient in being engaged as I was literally one Monday in Wick Sheriff Court, and the following Monday in Wigtown Sheriff Court, while others twiddled their fingers in Edinburgh.

The case which brought me before Sheriff Dobie involved a young soldier on leave from Germany who was charged under three sections of the old Road Traffic Act 1930: Section 4 (no licence), Section 11 (reckless driving) and Section 15 ("drunk driving").

The solicitor who instructed me had already tendered a plea of Guilty to section 4 before the trial. His client did not possess a driving licence.

I asked that this plea be withdrawn. The Depute Procurator-Fiscal no doubt wondering who was this young screwball of a junior counsel who made such a silly request allowed a plea of Not Guilty to be substituted. No doubt, he thought, even if he had to continue the case to bring evidence about that on another day it would be easily proved.

We proceeded to trial.

There was ample evidence to show that the car in question which had two male occupants had been driven in an erratic manner.

Drivers do not generally collide forcibly with lamp-posts on purpose. There was clear evidence from an eye-witness who identified my client without hesitation as the driver. There was clear evidence that my client, a young soldier on leave from Germany, was in no fit state through drink to be driving. The Crown case hung on being able to find corroboration of all this, or in particular corroboration of who the driver was.

There was then no statutory obligation on anyone to reveal whether he or she was the driver of a particular motor vehicle. So the Crown relied for corroboration on the evidence of another witness who had been at the scene of the crash. She pointed out my client as being amongst those present at the scene of the accident. The crucial part of her evidence was this:—

"From what he said I took it that he was the driver'"

I deliberately did not cross-examine her on this point. After all, since I did not know the answer, I might have found out to my disadvantage. All we had was her inference from a statement allegedly made by the accused. We did not have the statement itself. Accordingly, we did not know whether it was inculpatory or not.

Years later on the Bench I have often winced inwardly at unnecessary question put to witnesses by counsel and solicitors. Cross-examination I have always regarded as the supreme art of advocacy. It is a delicate tool in the hands of a craftsman and should never be wielded, as it so often is, like a hammer.

The courts today abound with well-fed hammer-throwers. Fortunately their clients do not know, as is so often the case, that it is their solicitor or counsel who has ensured their conviction.

Back to the case. No cross-examination on that point. I led no evidence. There are times when it is essential to put one's client in the witness box, but this was not one of them.

"When in doubt, keep him out" is a rough rule of thumb in criminal practice which more often than not yields a good result.

Sheriff Dobie however did not accept my submission that there was insufficient evidence in law to entitle him to convict. He duly found my client Guilty on both Section 11 and Section 15. I had argued that there was only one witness speaking to the fact that my client was driving. The so-called "corroboration" was only an inference from the facts spoken to, and we did not know what the man had actually said.

The Procurator-Fiscal, being satisfied with the result, dropped the charge on Section 4 of having no licence since he would have had to continue to another day to produce evidence on it. If someone is convicted of driving both "reckless" and "drunk" why bother about the question of a licence. The accused had been nailed.

Sheriff Dobie proceeded to fine my client and to disqualify him from driving, which, of course, Parliament had made obligatory.

There was only one course open which was duly taken—an appeal by Stated Case to the High Court in Edinburgh.

Sheriff Dobie, I believe, confided in someone that he had never "lost" in such an appeal and that this one was unlikely to succeed.

At the appeal the Crown was represented by the Solicitor-General W R Milligan QC (later Lord Advocate and a Court of Session Judge). The Lord Justice Clerk, Lord Thomson presided, assisted by Lord Patrick and another.

I proceeded to make the same submission as I had made to Sheriff Dobie. A short point. I could see that Lord Patrick was taking interest. It is only a personal opinion, but in my twenty-four years in Parliament House from 1949–1973 I would have placed him as one of the two best judges before whom I appeared. It was always well worth while for counsel to gain his ear. It had nothing to do with the result in this case, or the fact I had first met him on the grouse moor when I was still a schoolboy. The most important date in my father's sporting calendar was 12th August and on occasion Lord Patrick would join the party on the moors of which my father was a regular member, and I an occasional appendage.

Lord Patrick declared his position.

"Your plea is a highly technical one, Mr Bell. I have no sympathy with it but I think you are right". Sweet music in one's ears.

After the Bench had got into its usual huddle the Lord Justice Clerk announced that the Conviction would be quashed.

It was too late by then for the Crown to resurrect the charge that my client did not even have a licence. I can only hope that if he did not have one he celebrated his freedom to drive by acquiring one.

I never heard officially Sheriff Dobie's reaction to the result.

9

"HOWZATT"

The consumption of alcohol occupies much of the time of many who appear in Scottish Courts. I am not, needless to say, referring to the proclivities or the capacities of the Bench, Counsel or Solicitors many of whose members are unlikely to die of thirst . When the Faculty of Advocates was wont to hold an end of term dinner generally to celebrate a forthcoming marriage, I was reliably informed that the Albyn Restaurant in Edinburgh, the usual venue, sold more alcohol on such an occasion than at any other function throughout the year. There was of course always a verbal reminder from the Dean beforehand that no one should take a motor car.

It should of course be remembered that while many at the Bar have succeeded in reaching high office through the reckless use of both elbows, few have done so by the use of one.

While the "professionals" proceed at their own steady pace of intake through the year, in a manner which bears little relationship to the recommended maximum intake suggested by the medical profession, the "amateurs" tend to concentrate on festive periods such as Christmas and New Year. The more enthusiastic of them observe no discernible break from first heralding the approaching anniversary of the birth of Christ to launching the New Year well on the way.

Amongst their number still, sadly, are those who feel insecure if they do not have with them, while they stupefy themselves, a motor vehicle.

When the Courts re-open in January each year many of them are queuing up for the confessional. While all of them are regretful at having been apprehended, the majority are also truly regretful that they have committed an offence. Too late.

So it was, predictably that, on a January morning, I found myself facing a number of the chastened and blear-eyed.

The first had a blood alcohol count of 403; not the highest recorded but he might well have been dead. A lorry driver found slumped in his cabin at that time incapable of moving his limbs let alone driving a motor vehicle.

"This man" said the Procurator Fiscal appearing for the Crown "has one of the highest blood-alcohol counts I have experienced—403".

"It sounds more like a Bradman score" I replied.

He was duly fined and disqualified and left the Court with less money and, as so often sadly the additional penalty imposed elsewhere—no job.

Case number two was called. Before the Crown could say anything the defence solicitor leapt to his feet—he was Mr Ross Harper (now Professor Ross Harper).

"My Lord", he said "my client is also pleading guilty, but he is only in the Boycott class. His count is only 226".

"Boycott" I said "is perhaps an unfortunate word to mention in this context".

He, of course, was not only fined and disqualified, but I imagine he had also to pay Mr Harper.

10.

LAND AHOY

The Scottish Land Court which has a legal chairman of the standing of a Court of Session judge, and a number of lay members, deals with agricultural disputes, sits mainly in Edinburgh, but eight or nine times a year goes on circuit. It was presided over for many years by Lord Gibson. He was small of stature with, some said, commensurate grey matter and spoke precisely and haltingly in a quaint old fashioned Scots way, although by appearance he might more readily have adorned the pages of Dickens than of Sir Walter Scott.

To use moderate language his behaviour at times was eccentric. When appearing in front of His Lordship there was no point in becoming steamed up because he was unpredictable. One came to expect the most astonishing utterances, and to let them pass over without the blink of an eyelid. Had the media in those days thought that cultivation of land would be of a matter of public interest or even a matter of interest to the public, they might themselves have harvested a rich crop of stories...

It is said that on one trip to the Highlands and Islands, involving a passage by sea, His Lordship complained about the quality of transport provided for him. He opined grandly that, in his view, he might properly have been conveyed in a yacht. The highlander never slow to have a dig at pompous authority replied softly that if he had been a real Lord he would have had his own yacht.

I am told that on another occasion Ian Robertson QC (later Lord Robertson) was so upset at His Lordship's behaviour that he swept up his papers from the table in disgust to make a dramatic exit from the proceedings, only to find that when he tugged the door-handle to get out, it did not budge, and he was left stuck on the wrong side. This is not good theatre. At least, not of the kind intended.

On one occasion, I was appearing for an aggrieved landlord (it was generally after a hearing before His Lordship that a landlord felt aggrieved) in a dispute with his tenant. The tenant's record of wins to losses in this forum tended to be in the same ratio as those of Liverpool Football Club in its heyday. This of course, had nothing to do with His Lordship's socialist principles but of course to his evaluation of the evidence.

His Lordship suddenly, as was his wont interrupted my address at the close of the evidence, and I waited patiently to hear what was coming

His Lordship faltered but never failed on such occasions.

"Do-you-know" he said in his own particular hesitant way of speaking marking each individual word with a pause, and clearly pronouncing 'the' as 'thee' "that-the-Procurator-Fiscal-of-Campbeltown's-father-was-killed-by-the-only-bomb-which-landed-on-Campbeltown-during-the-war?" This was indeed sad if rather belated news.

I had first been in Campbeltown Sheriff Court and had then met the Procurator-Fiscal Ian Stewart in September 1952 when I managed to obtain an acquittal for a thirsty car-driver in front of that old scourge of the erring motorist, Sheriff James Frame. Frame had just been appointed to Campbeltown. Spurning the offer of the splendid traditional Sheriff's house beside the loch in this still feudal area he had as a good socialist applied to the local Council for a local authority house on the ground that he was a key worker. The acquittal which I obtained may have owed less to defects in the Crown case than to the mass of legal tomes which I had on the table. I had a hunch that the new Sheriff would not like to be appealed so soon.

"Not Proven" said he looking down at the mass of authorities.

But the speech I was making to Lord Gibson had nothing whatever to do with Fiscals or Campbeltown or bombs or wars.

I had not uttered a word to my knowledge remotely connected with any of them.

What had been triggered off in his mind, and how Lord Gibson came to make his interjection was, and still is, totally beyond my comprehension.

However, since counsel must at times seek to humour the bench and at all times to pick up the judicial train of thought, I informed him that I had had the pleasure of meeting the Procurator-Fiscal at Campbeltown and that I was deeply sorry to learn that he had lost his father in this way.

His Lordship nodded his approval of my sentiments and we proceeded immediately to return to the facts of the case and to deal with it as if we had never left it.

Very strange.

On another occasion we were listening to the evidence of a mole-catcher expounding on his professional skill. His Lordship eyed the man carefully. "Are you quite sure that you got rid of all the moles?" he enquired dubiously. "Of course, my Lord" replied the witness under oath. After the case, of course, the witness confided quietly "But I aye leave a few for breeding purposes". A wise mole-catcher would never render himself redundant.

Perhaps even more amusing was the day when Charles Johnston (later Sheriff Principal Johnston QC of South Strathclyde) who specialised to a degree in agricultural cases, was appearing also for a landlord.

The landlord had been visiting the farm which he owned, and of which he was seeking occupancy on the grounds that the tenant was not looking after the place properly.

The landlord was giving evidence and the merits were under discussion.

His Lordship suddenly turned to the landlord and asked:—

"And when you visited the farm did the farmer's wife give you a cup of tea?"

The startled landlord looked blank for a moment then recovering from his astonishment replied,

"Yes, My Lord as a matter of fact I did get a cup of tea."

His Lordship was not yet done.

"And was it a good cup of tea?" he enquired.

"Yes, yes it was quite a good cup of tea", replied the bewildered landlord.

At this point Charles Johnston had had enough. He interjected.

"My Lord," he said "I am not here to quarrel with the housewife's housewifery, but with the husbands husbandry."

11.

FIAT JUSTITIA

Lord Guthrie sat with stoic fortitude, hour after hour, while the dreary marriage tale unfolded. As a strict member and elder of the Presbyterian Church of Scotland and respecter of marriage he must have winced inwardly as all the minutiae of years of connubial misery were disputed by the warring couple.

Although a sufferer from arthritis, his concentration never lapsed. It was he who in another case felled the advocate who was relying on a bundle of old "hand-written" letters by asking when biro pens were invented. A question fatal to their authenticity. On a further occasion he sternly rebuked an Italian interpreter for failing to give an accurate translation.

For Counsel on both sides, who dissected the merits at length, there was at least the solace of the meter, attached to the Legal Aid Fund, which kept ticking away in the background. Protracted divorce cases then were ten-a-penny. The "cruelty" ones which I referred to as "Mrs Brady's bruises". The "adultery" ones which threw up strange scenes like the woman lying a deux on the bed wearing nothing but a smile while on a peg behind the door hung her wig. The bald truth and the bare truth indeed. Judges simply had to endure them.

The lady Counsel, Isobel Sinclair (later Sheriff Sinclair QC) a former journalist who brightened the Court with her scarlet lipstick and matching nail varnish—avante garde beyond belief in those days—who was appearing for the husband was making little headway with her cross-examination of the wife and now, in desperation, the protracted battle had moved from the bedroom to the kitchen.

Senior and junior Counsel on the other side sat silent. They were later, respectively, Lord Kissen and Lord Murray.

Lord Kissen, a shy generous and sensitive man of Polish Jewish extraction and a glutton for work, was at peace with the world. More so than when in his bachelor days he and a lady guest at a reception on board the paddle steamer "Waverley" were announced as "Mr and Mrs Kissen" In a flush of embarrassment he sought to have the mistake rectified.

A further message reached the assembled company:—"I have to inform you that the lady with Mr Kissen is not his wife".

Many of the party who did not know him must have puzzled over his marital status or his nocturnal activities. Lord Murray nephew of a former judge. Lord Birnam, and as a future Member of Parliament and Lord Advocate possessed of a rapid fire tongue must have found silence unbearable.

Until I had wandered in an idle moment into the Court I had been blissfully unaware of the high drama which was unfolding.

On entering, my ears rang.

I was positively startled to hear the flustered but penetrating voice of the lady advocate scream—with more than a hint of desperation—"And why did you give the tin of sardines to the cat?"

Why indeed? Being unaware of the relevance, unpossessed of the curiosity of the cat, and totally convulsed with laughter, I shot outside without waiting long enough to hear the answer. Indeed at the rate matters were proceeding, I might have lived through two or three of the cat's nine lives before finding out. Lord Guthrie may have been in pain, but the Legal Aid Fund was still solvent.

Why indeed did she—if she did—give the tin of sardines to the cat? You and I will never know. Nor will the cat.

And to think that the full panoply of the law in its awful, or is its awesome majesty was concerned to probe this crucial feline puzzle. I doubt if old Deuteronomy or even Gus could have provided the answer.

It is not, obviously, just every dog that has it day.

Fiat justitia.

12.

ONE LAW FOR THE RICH

"Daddy, it wasn't my fault".

As the London property developer who had made a quick kill in brick and mortar listened to his young son's appeal, his brow furrowed. The hard head which he had shown in his business dealings was not evident in the indulgence he displayed towards his youthful offspring.

It transpired that the son, who had been the recipient of an expensive motor car, had been touring in the Scottish Highlands. On a narrow road in Glen Nevis, under the shadow of the mountain, his car had come in minimal contact with one proceeding in the opposite direction driven by a Glasgow chartered accountant. Both vehicles had suffered slight damage, the drivers none. It was the sort of situation which, if happening in a city, before the days of road rage, would have involved a quick exchange of names and insurance companies, and found each driver driving away muttering to himself about the crass stupidity of the other. Even if the police had happened on the scene in a city, their advice might have been to tell both drivers to clear off quickly.

In Fort William, however, the incidence of crime was not sufficient to keep the police on a twenty-four hours stand by.

Moreover the accountant, who no doubt had done his sums quickly, and thought also about his no claims bonus, was away ahead of the young Londoner on points. The police were quickly summoned, statements taken, the vehicles examined, and no doubt a greater impact having been made by the voluble Scotsman on the question of fault, the young Londoner was charged with a contravention of Section 12 of the Road Traffic Act 1930—"careless driving".

Back home in London the sorrowing and pampered youth whined "Daddy, it wasn't my fault."

"Very well, my boy" said his father with a steely glint in his eye "we shall see about that".

Had the son pled guilty to the charge, the likely penalty at that time would have been a mere £5 fine and an endorsement of his licence. Many drivers would happily have left it at that.

Vindication of the Jones family honour, however, demanded that money should be no object in seeking to protect it. Father would see about that.

A well-known firm of London solicitors was instructed forthwith to bring their grey matter to bear. They may not have been aware as to the exact geographical location of Fort William, but they were at least conscious that it was not a frontier outpost in North America but that it was located somewhere in Scotland.

Very well.

They in turn having given anxious consideration to their clients' wishes, felt it incumbent to instruct a well-known firm of Edinburgh solicitors to delve deeper into the circumstances. It was indicated to Edinburgh that it was a matter of some importance to their client and that, in order to obtain "justice", there was to be no concern about the cost of the defence.

Re-assured by such comforting news, which would send a warm glow through any legal office, the Edinburgh solicitors decided, after mature consideration, that it was clearly a case for even further legal representation, namely the employment of a counsel experienced in road traffic cases.

Careless driving, I should interject, when there has been a collision and only one of the driver charged, is often a very difficult case in which to avoid a guilty verdict.

Motor cars do not of their own volition rush to lock horns.

It was at this stage, then, that I became involved as the third legal link in this weighty chain of defence. Some papers carefully wrapped and beribboned were sent, and I was briefed to proceed to Fort William Sheriff Court to defend on this onerous and anxious matter, and to meet with my young client.

The links of course were not yet quite complete; a fourth had to be forged in such a momentous case. Fort William is also some distance not only from London but also from Edinburgh, and it was found necessary, in addition, to instruct local solicitors to attend on counsel and to look after matters on the spot. Messrs Stewart, Rule & Co., a well-known firm in Inverness, were thus brought into the act. They had a branch office in Fort William. So, three sets of solicitors and one counsel all seeking to avoid a £5 fine.

This ship was not to be spoilt for a ha'pence worth of tar.

When I arrived in Fort William I was met by a soft-spoken Highland practitioner. He was clearly a man who would not have spent a shilling of his own money if sixpence would suffice. Almost his first words to me were a quiet aside in a soft Highland voice. "Mr Bell" he whispered confidentially "I think they've got more money than sense". This heresy of course was not repeated in public. He at least was well aware not only of the trivial penalty which might be involved, but of the difficulty in escaping it.

We proceeded to Court.

The prosecution was in the hands of the local Procurator-Fiscal, a pleasant fresh-faced man named Cuthbert of amiable demeanour with a shock of white hair. He was not quite old enough to be the sanctified one who helped to spread Christianity in Scotland but, nevertheless, gave the impression that he might have been happier doing that than harrying visiting motorists. He belonged to that old breed of country fiscals many of whom, having time on their hands, lived a relaxed life—fishing, shooting, bridge or golf—and as much time weekly in Court as it takes to play two sets of tennis at Wimbledon. Many were steeped in local lore.

It was Cuthbert who informed me with some pride during an interval that, although Fort William was remote, particularly not only to those from Edinburgh but also from the south, it should not be forgotten that the streets of Fort William had been lit by electricity before the streets of London. An irrelevant but, of course, an illuminating piece of information.

The principal Crown witness was, naturally, the driver of the other vehicle involved, the Glasgow chartered accountant. The Bench was occupied by Sheriff Reid Kerr whose first appointment had been to succeed Sheriff W R Walker at Banff but who, in order to fish different waters, had deserted the Deveron and had now moved "south" to replace Sheriff Cameron Miller who, in a hub bub of controversy, in Parliament, and without, had left to become Legal Adviser to British Rail in Scotland.

 I knew Robert Reid Kerr well since we had shared the same clerk when he was in practice at the Bar, the popular Gilbert McWhannell who having accumulated sufficient funds took himself to early retirement in Jersey. Not of course on ten per cent of my fees.

The accountant proceeded to give his version of what had transpired in Glen Nevis. His own driving had, of course, been impeccable. He was driving with reasonable care, at a moderate speed and keeping a proper look-out, when this young man who was doing none of these things had come in contact with his car. Fault was clearly one hundred per cent that of the youthful occupant of the other car. He was self-righteous, dogmatic and faintly aggressive. I noticed that the Sheriff was paying particular attention to him, and hoped that he was forming the same conclusion as myself.

Leaving the evidence aside, the accountant did not appear to be one of Scotland's best advertisements. He was meticulous, however, and took a long time to give his story. It struck me that instead of getting quickly to grips with him in cross-examination, and seeking to shrug off his evidence with one or two telling blows—my initial intention before I heard him—it might be better to string him along. To give him full reign to demonstrate the unpleasant facets of his character so that the Bench might develop for him the sort of antipathy which I had already acquired.

He did not fail me.

His aggressive voice, in what Somerset Maughan in one of his short stories was pleased to call the sing-song accents of Glasgow, continued to rasp and grate unevenly through the Court. Other witnesses followed, and the case which had started late had to be adjourned to the following day.

It had been a trying day in more ways than one for His Lordship. I also felt the need to be revived.

The pleasant hotel was quiet at that time of year and I repaired to it for a pre-prandial drink. I was a little surprised to find myself joined there soon by the presiding Sheriff who had happened by chance to seek a modicum of whisky in the same establishment. He was clearly glad of my company and seemed in no hurry to find his way home.

In a similar position on the Bench I should certainly have sought to avoid such an encounter at that stage, but it seemed politic to be pleasant to him. He clearly enjoyed the company, or perhaps it was just the whisky, and lingered until a late hour.

Lest a second eyebrow be raised I hasten to add that, throughout the evening, while we ranged on a large number of topics and consumed a large number of whiskies, never once did conversation turn to the case in which we were involved, except of course to the case of whisky.

Daylight came, (by this time the Sheriff had departed) and at 10.00am I returned to the Court. After some hours the case (that is the legal one) was almost finished and, after Cuthbert, I addressed his Lordship on the evidence. He was graciously receptive. Of course the crown evidence, particularly that of the accountant, was not reliable and fell far short of establishing my client's negligence. Of course. Indeed. There was only one possible verdict 'Not Guilty' which he duly announced.

A member of the public who had listened carefully throughout nodded his agreement with the decision. He was indeed satisfied but not delighted since he had never envisaged any other verdict. He was the London property man who himself had made the long journey to hear his son's case. Further expense, but well worth it to see justice triumph.

"You know" he said in expressing his thanks to me afterwards, and in a manner which indicated that he genuinely believed in the truth of his utterance, "It's a funny thing that if you can afford to pay for something, you usually get it"

I could not let things rest there. "Mr Jones", I replied, "no amount of money will guarantee in this country the successful defence of a criminal prosecution. You were merely paying to have a better chance of acquittal than some others in a similar predicament might have had".

I am not certain that he believed me.

13.

SURVIVAL OF THE FITTEST

Football players have training sessions. Cricketers take to the nets, and golfers seek the practice grounds. It is all a question of keeping fit to do one's job.

Advocates who depend on sharpness of mind and tongue, apart from reading the law, also do a bit of limbering up. The coffee room and the luncheon room in Parliament House may afford some space for flexing of the mind and the tongue muscles, but the real work-out takes place during the walk up and down Parliament Hall, under the Culross timbers where the last Scottish Parliament met in 1706, or before the stimulating glow of the robing room fire which is more recent and more transitory.

A warm posterior may well generate a quick opinion, although those who disagree with it may regard the posterior merely as the source of the opinion.

Conversation fell one morning, as we garrulous young juniors with little else to occupy ourselves than our own wit, toasted ourselves before the crackling logs to the accompaniment of a tear-jerking and traumatic problem: the splintering of a well-known solicitors' firm. Members of the Bar keep a watchful eye on Solicitors' firms. Nowadays a lot more of them seem to splinter.

Carstairs, Saughton and Bahamas were not the partners, but variously mentioned as the ultimate resting places for some of them.

The will to survive, it was agreed, was strong in all, and to some of the older survivors there was the added cushion of funds accumulated in practice over the years.

Concern and fellow feeling were felt for two younger partners, however, who had barely got a finger on one of the teats of the Legal Aid cow.

Someone had it that they were to launch a new firm together under the imposing name of Fairgrieve and Thomkins SSC.

Doubts were expressed about its survival.

"Well, one thing is certain", interposed a knowing one.

"David Fairgrieve will never starve".

The response came quickly and with feeling from Alistair Macdonald (later Sheriff Macdonald in Shetland) now sadly dead, a despiser of ball games who had once laboured in an office under Fairgrieve.

"No, not even if he has to eat Thomkins".

Fairgrieve to his further detriment you see, had once been a soccer referee as well as hard taskmaster.

The contemplation of anyone eating Thomkins filled us all and particularly Macdonald, a bon viveur, with gastronomic horror. It was he who declared fervently on one occasion amidst uproarious laughter that his Clerk would never accept an instructing brief which sent him anywhere for less than three and sixpence per day and a hot meal. I suspect also that a bottle of Chateau Neuf du Pape would have been part of the deal.

Even that he would have scorned if the instructing solicitor had mentioned rugby football. On one occasion he overheard a solicitor claim in praise that there was one thing about Edinburgh Academicals, they could kick.

Alistair turned on him in a flash "Good God" he expostulated "even a child in utero can kick".

Such were the gems of wit from able lawyers who fought to survive.

Alistair clearly was one of the fittest, and able to vindicate the clairvoyant powers of Robert Louis Stevenson by becoming Sheriff in Lerwick.

Tobermory of course by that time was no longer on the market, and despite sabre-rattling territorial claims to the island there had been no clamour to build a Sheriff Court on Rockall.

14.

LADY'S CHOICE

Charles Peeve was sacked summarily from his employment with the Gushforth Oil Company. (I need hardly say that both names are fictitious).

This was not to his liking and, from then on, neither was the Company. There was of course, in those days in a less caring society, no great rash of Industrial Tribunals to minister to the weak, so he felt it incumbent to take personal action.

Although it is not easy for one angry little gnat to interfere with the tread of a large elephant, this little gnat was determined to whine.

In his high-pitched fury he sent a hail of signals in every conceivable direction which, if not casting doubt on the lineage of senior management, made it plain to customers that this was not a company with which any respectable organisation, or indeed individual, should ever contemplate doing business.

As his campaign mounted, the company became irritated and decided that he better be silenced.

Accordingly, they raised an action of Interdict in the Court of Session that he should not "write, telephone or otherwise communicate or *"interfere with"* any customer or employee of the company, or any member of the families of any of them".

On first presentation, and without, of course, any representation of behalf of Mr Peeve, Interim Interdict was granted.

My brief, on behalf of Mr Peeve, was to seek to have this Interim Interdict withdrawn.

Since a number of the actions complained of were freely admitted this presented a little difficulty.

However, the case was put out before Lord Walker, a charming, quizzical and highly intelligent leg-puller of those Counsel who did not understand his sometimes oblique approach. There were not many judges approaching their eighties who padded about in "brothel-creepers" or should I say desert boots, dressed in sporty suits and drove a smooth Citroen. In fact only James Walker who apart from war service had spent thirty years as an Advocate 1915-1945 before taking "silk".

I had often sat as junior at his elbow when he was a senior Counsel, and knew his ways in and out of Court. I recall, for example, an evening when I was leaving a club to have dinner elsewhere and saw him arriving to join his ex-Gallipoli compatriots for a re-union.

"Archie, are you a member of this club?" (He was not).

"Yes of course" I replied.

"In that case", he said "You can buy me a drink".

He sniffed and described it as not the best Gin and French he had ever tasted and discreetly pulled rank, against club rules, by insisting on paying for it as well as one for myself. Or was it two?

"Clearly, my Lord", I began, "this interdict cannot stand. It is much wider than is necessary to protect the Gushforth Oil Company's interests".

Lord Walker said nothing.

"If one looked at it closely", I continued, "it would even prevent Mr Peeve from entertaining a young lady socially if, by chance, her father happened to be employed by the company". Lord Walker still said nothing.

"Interdict in this form was plainly far too wide and quite unnecessary for the protection of the company".

Lord Walker peered carefully at the wording. He was thinking of the young lady.

"It would stop him interfering with her" he said.

"Indeed, my Lord", I replied, "but surely that is a matter for the girl rather than for the Court".

Interdict was granted in more restricted terms which did not include the possibility of disappointing any young lady.

15.

OPEN DOOR

Any case, even at the end of weeks of evidence, may turn on one small point, but seldom dramatically so.

I had been briefed in the Court of Session to act for Jesners a well-known firm of Jewish car dealers in Glasgow. It had been alleged by a customer that he had paid them in cash for the purchase of a motor vehicle, and this they strenuously denied.

The case was heard by Lord Mackintosh and because of pressure of space at the time, in the Second Division courtroom of the Court of Session.

I was on my own as a junior. The other side was represented by Gordon Stott QC (later Lord Advocate and Lord Stott), and Ewan Stewart, then a junior, (later Lord Stewart).

The customer described how, in an office, the whole sum of money involved had been counted out and handed over to the Jesner representative in notes.

Lord Mackintosh was taking his own careful stock of the man's account of the transaction.

Even if Lord Mackintosh were to believe him, of course that would not be the end of the case. The vital corroboration would have to be produced.

Gordon Stott known affectionately as 'Goofy' by the junior Bar, most of whom had a high respect for his ability, had a mind as sharp as a razor's edge and would never have allowed them to proceed to Court without some ostensible corroboration. Whether it was to be believed would be a matter for the judge.

The "supporting" witness entered the box confidently. He described how he had accompanied his friend to Jesners' office.

When his friend had gone inside, he had waited outside the door. The door was ajar, and through the open space he had seen his friend count out and hand over the money.

So far so good.

My information, however, seemed to differ from that of the witness. I began to cross-examine him.

"Was this door just an inch or two open?"

"No, it was wider than that" replied the witness.

"Perhaps six inches or a foot?"

"No just a little wider" he said. After all he had to satisfy the court that there was sufficient space for him to have a good view of the transaction.

Having got him to open the door that far I posed my next question:—

"My information, Mr Smart (fictitious), is that this door, once opened, was on an automatic closing device. Have you anything to say about that?"

He was totally flummoxed. He stood silent. He had never thought of that and was not in a position to dispute it. It was too late even to "help" his friend had he been minded to do so, by suggesting that he had X-ray eyes and had seen through the door.

Lord Mackintosh took the point. Jesners won quickly and comfortably.

16.

BITTER EXPERIENCE

A naval court-martial is a forbidding tribunal. A row of officers sits there in judgement, arms laced with gold braid bands, and grim faces beneath their "scrambled egg" caps.

Admiral Byng might have corroborated this, but of course only for a brief spell after his appearance before one. He was shot.

It can never be a pleasure for officers of the senior service to act as judge and jury in a matter concerning one of their own number. Despite their appearance, they are a reasonable and human body. But discipline is discipline and, in the Royal Navy as I know from personal experience, of paramount importance.

My client was a young lieutenant. He had not mislaid an aircraft carrier, or run a battleship on to the rocks. In fact he was in the Paymaster Branch as denoted by the white stripes then accompanying the two straight rings on his sleeve, and at the time was acting as Captain's Secretary in a shore establishment.

He was a member of a well-known brewing family, and about to go on leave. He little knew what he was brewing up for himself.

Like a lot of people who deal with paper work, he had an "IN" tray and an "OUT" tray. The general idea, I am told, is to try to arrange that the former is empty and the latter is full.

Lieutenant Bitter (not of course his real name but the source of the family wealth) had not managed to achieve this. In fact one could say that he had almost achieved the reverse position. A huge pile lay in his "IN" tray. It was obvious to him that if he were to get his own priorities right—namely to shoot off on leave—he would have to do something quickly with this nasty tell-tale heap.

He fixed on a simple answer. He merely lifted the entire stack of papers in the "IN" tray and no doubt with a single grunt of satisfaction deposited them all in the waste-paper basket. "Hmm, that's that" you could almost hear him say.

Breathing a sigh of relief that he had "dealt" with all the work in hand he left his office and went off for a spot of leave.

There are those who send out letters to create work for themselves. There are those who do so prompted by commercial instinct. It would be more expensive to sift out who might be an appropriate recipient than to mail the community at large. Thus QC's and judges may be offered legal advice by post and perhaps a male octogenarian will be proffered help on how to cope with his first pregnancy.

It may be that on other occasions nothing might have happened. After all, people whose delight is to circulate or distribute "bumf" cannot be optimistic enough to expect an answer every time they do. The people who bombard me with junk mail should be able to confirm this. In any event, something should be done to discourage them.

This time there was trouble. Big trouble. The tray had not been full of junk mail.

Amongst the papers so generously heaped in the waste-paper basket was a signal from the Admiral. The Admiral had expected a response.

When the Admiral did not receive a response he thundered off a second communication, this time a broadside, seeking an explanation for the silence at the other end. To those still on duty it was as if a 16 inch shell (the largest then on offer by the Royal Navy) had whistled past their heads. Everyone moved quickly to 'Action Stations'.

After a hurried and frantic search the original signal was discovered, but not quickly, in the huge pile of paper in the Captain's Secretary's waste-paper basket. No doubt by this time Lieutenant Bitter was sitting relaxed with a pink gin wowing some starry eyed filly in more congenial surroundings that did not remind him of a life on the ocean wave.

He was not to remain there long. The wires hummed and he was hurriedly recalled and, being unable to provide a satisfactory explanation to his immediate superior, was promptly put on a court-martial. Hence his appearance, and mine on his behalf, before this frosty quartet.

By the time they had totted up all his alleged misdemeanours there were fifteen charges in all.

For eleven of these the prosecuting officer relied on affidavit evidence. That is to say that he produced sworn statements from a number of people who were not present at the hearing, relating to the charges as to what they might have said had they been present.

I immediately objected to the admission of these on the grounds that I was unable to cross-examine a statement, and there was no way of testing the strength—or the weakness—of the allegations which were made in it.

To my surprise, my objection was upheld.

Eleven of the fifteen charges were struck out. For the rest I had to struggle and to rely on argument. There could be no total "escape". In the end, however, he was only found guilty on two of the fifteen counts.

Although this was a lay tribunal (so far as the law is concerned) they had acted with complete fairness.

The Lieutenant was not to be shot, to suffer loss of seniority or to be dismissed ship. He received a reprimand. This, I hope did not interfere too seriously with his naval career. I would doubt however if he became an Admiral. More likely Lieutenant Commander RN (retd).

He had, however, dare I say it, learned from bitter experience.

17.

DEATH AT THE ROADSIDE

Road traffic again took me to the borders—this time to Hawick which sadly no longer boasts a Sheriff Court. My client who appeared on indictment was charged with culpable homicide (what in England is called manslaughter).

The case involving a well-known local businessman had aroused not only a great deal of interest but a great deal of indignation.

The alleged facts were not such as would commend themselves to the sympathies of a jury and a local jury at that. The story was that my client had been out drinking on a Saturday night. By eleven p.m. having consumed more than was good for him—or even for several others as well—he jumped into his expensive sports car.

With limited vision and impaired co-ordination he sped downhill in the direction of his next engagement. This was to be with a lady who was not his wife. It was alleged that he was detained outside her house unscrewing the broken stem of his wing mirror which had been left shattered and had fallen at the scene of the crash. Unfortunately while driving he did not see in the darkness, two local men who were wending their way uphill on foot. He struck them both with bone-crunching force. One was killed outright. The other was thrown over the bonnet and spent a long and painful period in hospital.

When the trial was called before Harald Leslie QC the Sheriff-Principal (later Lord Birsay, Chairman of the Scottish Land Court) the public benches were packed with local spectators as well as potential jurors.

Before television had reared its first crop of couch potatoes, people had to seek their own entertainment. What better than to have a real live drama on your own doorstep with a local actor in the leading role. On such occasions the local Madame

DeFarge might well be squeezed in between a member of the Church Women's Guild and a member of the Women's Rural Institute or even one who wanted to take part in the Common Riding. Not all of course would be able to savour the grisly or spicy details, but those attending could pass them on with relish to a wider but equally curious audience who were unable to attend.

Had they known what was in my mind the spectators might have stayed at home.

My motion was that the trial should be adjourned to a later date. The inconvenience to the Crown, to the police, to the witnesses, in fact to almost everyone caused by an adjournment would be considerable. One had to weigh this up and put it in the balance before making such a motion. I was not popular. I have never, however, worried too much on that account or shrunk from doing what I thought was right because some might whisper and others might bawl. Popularity in itself is not my yardstick of social acceptability. If you don't believe me just look at the faces which appear on "Top of the Pops".

The reason I gave for making the motion made some beg to wonder if I had temporarily lost my sanity. It was not just the fact that an essential witness who had been cited was absent unavoidably on the ground of illness. It was the fact that the witness in question was the principal Crown witness, the surviving man on whom prosecution hopes were pinned who had been thrown over the bonnet and who, by that time, was still in hospital and might not be thought to be the most necessary witness for the defence.

My motion was successful and an adjournment was granted. This of course merely postponed the whole business but, in the event, altered the whole situation radically. The show left town. We were moved out of Madame DeFarge's territory and towards a jury whose knowledge of the facts might owe more to the evidence than to the local bush telegraph.

The trial proceeded, this time at Jedburgh Sheriff Court in front of the late Sheriff D I McLeod who had taken office at a time when it was difficult to persuade any member of the Bar to become a Sheriff unless he were cash strapped or of independent means and in search of country life; an interesting contrast to later when I was privy to reading a list of thirty-five applicants for one vacancy in Glasgow.

The other important difference naturally was the presence this time of the unfortunate survivor of the accident.

I felt genuinely sorry for the poor man. He had been brought from hospital to give evidence. He must still have been suffering both physically and mentally. He was still so ill that he was brought into Court on a stretcher and remained there recumbent while giving evidence. I can assure you that it is no pleasure for Counsel to have to interrogate in such circumstances.

The reason why I wanted him to be present and to give evidence was this. He and his companion according to my information had also had a "night out". I felt so sorry for him, but my primary duty was not to him, but to my client.

Step by step I led him in cross-examination gently through his movements that evening. He was a decent man, and an honest man. He admitted that he and his deceased companion had also been out drinking.

Crucially, he eventually admitted that he and his deceased companion were so drunk that they had been staggering on the road in the face of oncoming traffic. The Crown, had other evidence, however, irrespective of his condition and that of his companion that suggested my client was not blameless.

At the close of the Crown case I asked that the charge of culpable homicide be not allowed to go to the jury on the grounds that there was insufficient evidence before them to entitle them to convict. If there is any reasonable argument in such a situation it has to be put forward by the defence. There is nothing to lose. Particularly since I had by then a sneaking suspicion that the bush telegraph might have breached the walls of evidence and that this local jury might also be looking for a pound of flesh.

My argument was upheld although frankly, I am not certain that on the Bench I would have made the same decision. We play to win, however, when defending, and my plea had been put forcibly.

My client eventually stepped from the dock a free man. Everywhere there was hubbub and the buzz of conversation.

The first job was to seek to have my client rescued from the clutches of the vultures who were waiting for him outside, reporters, photographers and fellow citizens. I have always enjoyed good relations with the press and am well aware that the press do a useful job on many occasions in highlighting and bringing to the attention of the public matters which happen in a Court of Law. They are not always, as a late colleague Sheriff-Principal Robert Reid QC described them to me, as "maggots waiting for a corpse to feed on". My client however was desperate to avoid the centre of the stage.

With a little ingenuity he was smuggled from the court without so much as one picture being achieved by a single press photographer, a fact which would not have pleased a few editors. Back in the peace of my hotel he expressed his gratitude at the outcome.

All was not yet over.

Next day to my astonishment the Daily X printed a

photograph of him with a broad grin on his face. The caption said "Smiling George K after his trial".

There was local outrage. People could not believe that any man who had been involved in the death of one man and the maiming of another, even without guilt, would be as callous as to appear publicly immediately after his acquittal with a grin on his face. The public did not know that he had not done so. It was, however, the obvious inference to anyone who looked quickly at the newspaper.

The public were not concerned with the fact—if there be a difference—that the caption had said "smiling George K after his trial" as opposed to "George K smiling after his trial".

At first we were at a loss to know how the photograph had come to be published.

The matter was soon resolved and very simply.

It transpired that the newspaper in question, refusing to be "cheated" of a picture had managed to obtain a photograph of a happy local group taken some time earlier at a wedding where my client was a guest.

They had simply cut out the rest of the group, blown up his photograph and produced a picture of the acquitted man as he had appeared on a previous and happier occasion, with a smile on his face.

Any comment on this I am glad to leave to the reader.

18.

JOINING THE CLUB

In England the motorist on a drink charge might be dealt with by Magistrates, or elect to be tried by a jury which gives well-known public figures, if they have popular appeal, perhaps a greater chance of acquittal. The ancient and "sacred right" of the Englishman to avail himself of a jury in such cases would appear to a Scotsman merely as an unnecessary additional expense and source of delay and give no reason to suggest that justice was more likely to prevail if the verdict were to be entrusted to a bunch of amateurs rather than to one professional. This is not to suggest that jury trial should not continue for the most serious charges.

Thus Bill Edrich, the cricketer, whom I met every summer was able to tell me of his own "escape" and also of being bidden to a party given by Terry Thomas who had been in a similar predicament but who had also elected to go to a jury where guests were handed a pin on arrival to stick into a cake covered with marzipan blue policemen to celebrate another acquittal.

In Scotland those similarly charged do not enjoy the same luxury. and the odd privilege when charged of being able to decide who would try them. Rich or poor, illustrious or notorious all appear in front of a single judge, the Sheriff.

In the fifties the ever mounting number of bibulous motorists appearing in front of him eventually resolved Sheriff Prain sitting in Perth to announce drastic action. The county was prosperous, the farming community in particular was then prosperous, and there was a regular procession of farmers appearing in front of him whose horses no longer, as in former days, found their own way home from the market pulling carts with their well-refreshed masters on board. These had been replaced by Bentleys and other expensive vehicles "controlled", to use the word loosely, by their owners.

Bentleys do not have the same homing instincts as horses. They have to be steered.

Accordingly, his Lordship announced one day that in view of the enormous increase in the number of cases involving drink and driving, he proposed to start sending those found guilty of driving while under the influence of drink to prison. So in Scotland unlike as in England, the soft cushion often afforded by a jury was not available. Despite this dire warning, many were soon in Sheriff Prain's net, and many received salutary short sharp treatment—a month inside.

So the local rhyme ran:—

"Thirty days hath September,

April, Prain and November".

Distress was caused to some socially, but the matter lay in their own hands. In many criminal matters—I hasten to add that I would not say all—increased penalty does begin to have a salutary effect, and the number of convictions to drop. My qualification is important since I do not wish to divert to a debate with the Howard League of Penal Reform.

They would not be moved by the story that in 1939 when Hitler was touring the Third Reich before embarking on war to see that civil affairs were in good order, the only worry in Hamburg, according to the Mayor, was that there were too may burglars. The Führer, it was said, immediately issued a decree that the next six persons found guilty of burglary were to be shot. It is said that the incidence of burglary thereupon dropped dramatically.

Criminals face three main risks—apprehension, conviction and incarceration. The greater the probability of all three coinciding, the less likelihood there must be of fewer crimes being committed.

Unfortunately some surprising victims came into the net, not of course at the risk of the firing squad, but nevertheless at risk of incarceration. Despite a vigorous and skilful defence, the brother of a former Prime Minister found himself awaiting sentence on a drink-driving charge

The law of course could not make an exception for him so, like many others, he found himself having a month's "rest" in Perth Prison. This, notoriously, housed some of the worst criminals in Scotland and there were no first class cabins aboard.

When he came out, his friends affected to be vastly amused by the whole affair. The script is not verbatim, but from what I was told ran a bit like this:—

"Tell me old chap what was it like?" No response.

"Had a good holiday?" No response.

"Come on, what was it really like?" This time he was moved to speak.

With true aristocratic aplomb he answered with a dismissive air:—

"Oh a bit like the Liberal Club" he replied "Only the food was better!"

I do not know what his reactions would have been to the reported comments of the prisoners at Strangeways, some of whom after the most destructive riots there stated that life in prison was ideal.

Where else, they said, could you obtain, free of charge, three meals a day and a roof under your feet.

19

LINGERING SUSPICION

It is, I suppose, less difficult now, with the increasing inquisitiveness of the media, for the general public to appreciate the suspicion aroused in lawyers that outside influences may occasionally interfere with the due process of the law. It may, of course happen and in this the media, despite outside criticism often perform a useful service. No system of justice is perfect. Those who prosecute, Crown counsel or any Procurator-Fiscal would be able to tell you. Anyone who has defended likewise. Obvious obstacles to the proper administration of justice are a witness's sudden self-imposed amnesia or, in more sinister fashion, the pressures brought to bear by bribes on one hand, or intimidation on the other. Sometimes one is left with a lingering suspicion even at the end of a trial that something may have been amiss. This also in the context that "proof," as Lord Carmont was wont to remind us, "is only a high degree of probability".

The law at times may deal in logical exclusions e.g. *HMA* v *Withers* a murder case where, since accident and suicide had been eliminated as the cause of death, the only remaining possibility was murder, but it does not deal in mathematical certainties. Put in perspective thousand upon thousand of cases are dealt with honestly and conscientiously in a manner which gives no cause for concern by the public.

Since no system of justice is perfect, it is right that the public and the media should express concern if they think that there has been a miscarriage of justice. The number of recent cases where an Appeal Court in England has quashed a conviction because new evidence has come to light or it was thought that it was "unsafe" to convict on the original evidence are not an indictment of "British" justice as a whole. They merely highlight aspects of the administration of justice in England, not in Scotland which of course also on occasion may have its problems.

What of course the public should bear in mind is that if it is held on appeal in England that it was "unsafe" to convict in a particular case, this is not to declare categorically that the accused have been proved innocent of the charge against them.

I remember, however, a well known English QC who was defending in the murder trial of a notorious member of the London underworld. He was said, rightly or wrongly, to point out at conference that the chances of acquittal for his client would be very much higher but for one stumbling block; the witness XY. I shall not, of course, name the counsel or the case.

This alleged appraisal at the pre-trial conference had apparently been noted carefully and was said to have been conveyed to some of the accused's friends. Whether by coincidence or otherwise, the story had it that the body of XY was found soon afterwards in circumstances which left no doubt that he had not died from natural causes. His absence from the trial may have contributed to the accused's acquittal. I put it no higher.

The worst inference however would be that Counsel had unwittingly signed the man's death warrant. Whether such an inference would have been justified, I cannot tell. Frightening. The law cannot with certainty guarantee a true verdict in every case.

A less sinister case which aroused some considerable suspicion amongst a small part of the population of Lanarkshire took place in Airdrie Sheriff Court on 17th and 18th June 1953.

The suspicion arose because, in some parts of Scotland, particularly in the West-Central industrial belt, people are not always by instinct well-disposed to those who pray—if and when they do—under the auspices of a different church. In this part of Lanarkshire with which we are concerned there was a distinct

Protestant–Roman Catholic divide. The name Monklands now springs to mind. They are of course by definition all Christians and ought to love their neighbours.

Two men were charged with conspiracy to defraud the National Health Service, a chemist (Protestant) and a medical practitioner (Roman Catholic). The "plot" was alleged to be as follows:— that the doctor wrote a large quantity of "phoney" prescriptions in the names of patients on his list. They were not, of course, given to the patients nor were they told about them. The chemist received, but did not dispense, these prescriptions. Then a large claim for remuneration was lodged by the chemist with the National Health Service on the basis that they had been dispensed. The chemist and doctor came to a financial arrangement over the proceeds. Quite simple.

As may be appreciated, witnesses do not always say what one wants them to say, or what previously they have indicated they will. I was always amused as a Scottish counsel when I received from England the equivalent of what we call in Scotland a precognition—a summary beforehand of a witness's supposed evidence, headed "John Bloggs Will Say". This seemed to me the height of optimism.

The chemist, a Protestant was defended by myself (fortuitously born a Protestant). The doctor—a Roman Catholic, was defended by Lawrence Dowdall (fortuitously, I assume, born a Roman Catholic).

Andrew Nixon, the Procurator-Fiscal (later PF in Aberdeen) had cited a host of Crown witnesses. Presumably each was meant to depone in the clearest terms, when a prescription was produced in Court bearing his or her name, that no such prescription had ever been issued to that particular patient.

Then rumour had it that the Crown might be in difficulties. The patients were virtually all Roman Catholics. Nasty gossip was floating about, presumably disseminated falsely by some evil and bigoted Protestants, that a priest, not the parish priest then in the area, but one who knew the area and most of the patients, had taken it upon himself to pay a visit before the trial to a number of the patients who had been cited as witnesses.

The evil suggestion alleged to have been put in their minds by him was that perhaps, after a long interval, their recollection might not be too clear as to whether or not the doctor had given them a prescription on the material date, and that they might bear this in mind. Possibly a member of the household might have required medication. It might be to their doctor's advantage if this were so.

Had this been true of course it would have been a serious attempt to pervert the course of justice in a manner and on a scale unique in the experience of many seasoned lawyers.

For a day and a half the Crown led witness after witness. Time and again the witness was asked if he or she had ever received a prescription from doctor X on the date appearing on the production put before him or her.

Time and again, witness after witness stated that he or she "might have done so". It was a long time ago, and difficult to remember, but the witness could not say categorically that such prescription had not been dispensed. This was not what the Crown meant them to say. Amnesia is neither infectious nor contagious.

There was a sudden interruption, however, in the current pattern of the evidence, which until then must have caused despair to the Crown, and was so innocuously delivered from a defence point of view that it involved practically no cross-examination by Dowdall or myself.

An elderly Orcadian woman walked firmly into the witness box. She was a Protestant and had little local connection. She was also the picture of health. She declared in loud and emphatic terms that this prescription which bore to have been issued in her name by doctor x she had never seen or requested. She and her family enjoyed excellent health, and she categorically stated that she had never at any time had cause to receive any prescription. In fact, she seemed insulted at the very suggestion that she might require medical treatment. As they say in Ireland, she must have been a very healthy woman when she died.

The implications from this particular piece of evidence if true, were clear. The prescription which bore to have been issued by the doctor must be a "phoney".

In a less forthright way one or two other witnesses also stated that they had not received prescriptions. The general pattern of amnesia however, was resumed until, by lunch-time on the second day, the Crown case was outwardly in tatters and the poor Procurator-Fiscal who looked in need of a prescription for himself announced that he would "have to consider his position" over the luncheon interval.

It was obvious that he was going to capitulate.

There had, at the start of the second day been another small incident which had nothing to do with the case.

At 10.15am or so a telegram arrived addressed to myself from my then wife's sister, who was then on the stage, announcing an addition to my family. It simply said, repeating the title of a well known play at that time, "To Dorothy a Son". Dorothy was the name of my wife. My instructing solicitor, Jim McClure of Findlay McClure and Co in Glasgow, with a wicked grin gave it to the Sheriff Clerk who quickly transmitted it to the Bench.

The Sheriff ("Barney") Stevenson, nodded and beamed down his benevolent congratulation.

We adjourned.

It has never been my custom at any time during the course of a day in court to consume any alcohol even in the smallest quantity. On this occasion Lawrence Dowdall and McClure, neither of whom were total abstainers, seemed to think that this was not a time to lend succour to the temperance movement. Although my father and grandfather had been Elders of the Kirk, I concurred.

It was not only the Sheriff Court in Airdrie which was then old. The only place there to have luncheon was the old Commercial Hotel which, if rated in "stars" I might grudgingly have awarded a *tiny* meteorite. We repaired there at once, however and proceeded modestly between 1pm and 1.45pm to celebrate Kenneth's birth. I cannot recollect that we troubled the chef.

Before 2.00pm we returned promptly and in good order to Court.

In those days Courts generally sat promptly. Everyone then assumed that punctuality was important. Thousands of hours of judicial time could now be saved if this simple practice were followed to-day.

On our return we were immediately greeted by the Procurator-Fiscal's announcement that, in view of the course of the evidence led, he did not intend to proceed further. Acquittal.

The chemist and the doctor were both found NOT guilty.

It was indeed a day with a double cause to celebrate, but whether the court victory was entirely due to the forensic skill of Dowdall and myself is one which leaves me with a lingering doubt.

There was certainly considerable dismay amongst some of the local population at the verdict. Mostly Protestants I suspect.

Lawrence Dowdall incidentally then Glasgow's top criminal law practitioner, was not only an astute but a thoughtful and kindly man. Our next meeting took place soon thereafter when he instructed me to appear in two cases at the next sitting of the High Court in Glasgow. Children, you see as he knew, and as most Roman Catholics have more cause to know than Protestants, can be expensive.

20.

SEQUEL

Shortly afterwards I was instructed to appear with John Wheatley QC (later Lord Wheatley) as his junior in another case in Airdrie Sheriff Court. It was, oddly, also a case of fraud on the National Health Service. The accused—yes, indeed—another Roman Catholic medical practitioner. The facts were such that Wheatley immediately advised that there would have to be a plea of Guilty, but that a strong plea could be put up in mitigation.

Again the Sheriff was "Barney" Stevenson. A very pleasant man, in his day a first class opening bat on the cricket field for Edinburgh Academicals, it was said that he often found passing sentence a problem. What person who sits on any bench from the highest to the lowest could not say the same? Even with the gratuitous advice proffered by the press, the trade unions, the social work department, the psychiatrists, the politicians and anyone suffering from innate prejudice, personal emotion or indigestion.

Sentencing is in my view any judge's most difficult job. One passes sentence always in the knowledge that while some members of the public will applaud, others may be outraged or aggrieved. So be it. It should however be remembered that, as in most walks of life the professionals know best and that they have two enormous advantages over the belly-achers—they are objective, and they know the whole story.

It was said of "Barney", no doubt untrue, that if he was satisfied by lunch-time as to what sentence he should pass he retired to his chambers over the interval and consumed a boiled egg. If he had doubts he went home during the break and consulted his wife as to what he should do.

Wheatley spoke without pause for some forty-five minutes. It was an eloquent and persuasive plea. Barney listened without interruption.

When Wheatley finished it was long before the luncheon interval. It was neither time for Barney to chew on his boiled egg, nor time to consult his wife. A decision had to be made.

No doubt conscious of local indignation about the previous case, and with the full knowledge that this second doctor had admitted his guilt, Barney decided though not a harsh man, that an exemplary sentence was required. Sixty day's imprisonment. It would not be the end for the doctor. He would still have to face the General Medical Council. The sentence was a surprise to everyone.

Before leaving Airdrie I had already been instructed by Messrs Black, Cameron and Campbell Solicitors, Glasgow, through Gray, Muirhead and Carmichael WS, in Edinburgh to draft a Bill of Suspension which was the appropriate mode of appeal.

Again in the Appeal Court I sat at John Wheatley's elbow as he prepared to make his general address on behalf of the doctor, this time before the formidable High Court array of Lord Justice-General Cooper, Lord Carmont and Lord Russell.

It was 12.35 p.m. when Wheatley rose to speak. He delivered himself until 1.00 p.m., when the Court rose for the luncheon interval. A number of people in the public galleries were seen to be praying—"more things are wrought by prayer"..... The address, again eloquent, was getting absolutely no change out of the Bench. They sat stony faced.

I cannot conceive of what happened during the interval when discussion may have taken place between the judges as they sat munching together. Lord Cooper certainly did not consult his wife. He was a bachelor.

As a participant, however, it was astounding.

After lunch I felt like a rugby player who had been involved in kicking uphill against the wind in the first half and now found that the slope and the elements were in our favour.

Wheatley continued to animadvert—a favourite word of his —and this time was making progress. There were the odd sympathetic murmurs from the bench. Eventually the whistle blew.

Their Lordships quashed the sentence of imprisonment and substituted a fine.

I never discovered what "Barney" thought about it, or what sentence—given the opportunity—his wife might have thought appropriate.

21.

THE QUICKNESS OF THE HAND

In another chapter I have used the expression "lingering suspicion" but it also brings to mind a different type of case.

The case was one of attempted murder and took place in the High Court at Edinburgh. It involved a dispute amongst some "hard" men of the Edinburgh underworld. One, in particular, was displeased at the close attention given by another to a lady who enjoyed not only his favours, but also his affections. The two as you maybe aware do not always go together.

It is well-known (as I have indicated elsewhere in relation to a young car thief) that the penalties which members of the public might impose given the chance, are often far more severe that any judicial body would impose. As a professional you only have to boggle at what happens in "kangaroo" courts or those set up by trade unions or sporting bodies.

When it comes to the hard men of the underworld, they don't mess about; they are quick to dispense their own "justice". The aggrieved here acted promptly. Unknown to him, the errant Lothario was tried in absence by an angry man acting as both judge and jury, and was about to face the same individual cast in the sinister role of executioner. A friend went along also to see that justice was meted out.

The sentence was a straightforward one. They would discharge a loaded shotgun into his private parts.

You can imagine Lothario's feelings when he was rudely shaken and awoken in the early hours of the morning, had the bedclothes pulled back, and a loaded double-barrelled gun presented at the lower part of his body. There was no opportunity given to enter into diplomatic negotiations or to make a plea in mitigation. The weapon was promptly discharged.

Unless you have heard of the man who could not even hit the proverbial bovine on the backside with a banjo while holding its tail you will not readily grasp that it is possible, outside of Hollywood of course, to fire from a short distance and to miss the target. To be precise, the gunman missed the "bull", if that be the appropriate word, but he managed to score an "inner". The genitalia, were bypassed, but the victim was severely wounded in the groin.

Thus I came to be briefed to defend his alleged assailant on a charge of attempted murder.

The police had done their homework. The two intruders used to visit a public house in Jamaica Street, Edinburgh, just behind Heriot Row. The public house, if not within judicial knowledge, was within much judicial sight. The street of course has now been demolished with the result that there are fewer wife beatings or Alsatian dogs in the area. This was the old Northern Bar, later re-named The Red Dragon and ultimately when remodelled named The Purple Onion (at the opening of which I was invited as a guest to attend). It is now, I understand, called something else.

Information was said to have been obtained there of the plan of attack—I cannot vouch for this—from a lady who was a regular patron and often sat there knitting (like a latter day Madame DeFarge) as she consumed her glass of stout. She ran a nearby second hand clothes shop under the name of Madame Doubtfire. It was often suggested that some of the Bar, or more particularly their wives, were patrons of hers. Haute couture was not the companion of many Faculty wives in those days, and Madame Doubtfire, the joke ran, was able to provide at modest cost for those who eschewed the plunging neckline or the short skirt.

The Crown had sufficient evidence to go to trial, but again the vital question of corroboration loomed up. If the jury were to reject an alleged statement made by the accused I felt that the omens were good.

The crucial police witness went into the box to speak to the "confession".

Needless to say, I hung on his every word.

It transpired that he had arrived with his pencil and notebook at 10.00pm in an unlit tenement, an old property near Holyrood Palace popularly known as Dumbiedykes. This was his evidence:— As he reached the door of the house inside which were the accused and his lady, a dialogue began, not after the manner of Plato, but in the end more of a soliloquy.

Just as the officer poised his notebook in the darkness, with his sharp pencil at the ready the accused began to speak— quickly, very quickly.

"Do you want me to f—ing tell you about it?" was his opening query according to the officer, (coming from my client this would have been a polite enquiry).

"Aye, tell me about it" replied the lady. ("It" was the alleged attack on the victim of the shotgun).

"Well, I'll f—ing tell you about it".

According to the officer the accused then described in detail to his female companion how he had gone to the victim's house and shot him. This was not just powerful evidence. If believed it was an admission which would destroy totally any defence.

The officer read out the whole of the accused's alleged statement of confession on which he had so happily chanced. The notes of course, said the officer had been made at the time.

I asked to see the officer's notebook. There it all was, if not quite in copperplate, in a clear, bold, legible hand. I could not credit it.

When I addressed the jury I told them that this writing could not possibly be genuine, nor the witness truthful. I showed them the notebook. I invited them when they retired to ask to see with the judges permission, the entry in the notebook, to examine it closely, and each to answer the question "could what you see written down here have been taken down in long hand in such perfect writing at 10.00pm in a darkened close?". If the jury disbelieved the evidence they could only acquit my client.

The coincidence that the officer stated that he arrived at the exact moment this "confessional" began, I told them, was an additional reason for rejecting the evidence. A quite incredible coincidence I suggested. This was not just a matter of telling the jury. I believed, actually believed rightly or wrongly that it, was "phoney". But such judgements are not for me. They found him guilty.

My client was sentenced to seven years' imprisonment.

When the regular crowd of press reporters buzzed round after the verdict one of them, who confronted me, he may have been from the *Daily Express*, was laughing all over his face.

"Do you know" he said "at the speed the policeman read that statement out, I could hardly get it down in short hand". And he was sitting down. And writing in daylight.

I do not know whether my client was guilty or not, but certainly amongst the press at least there was a lingering suspicion about the one vital part of the evidence which secured a conviction.

22.

SAFE IN THE ARMS OF THE LAW

Somehow I seem to hark back to the track of "lingering suspicion". This brings me to the Princes Street bank robbery in which I defended.

Some rebuilding (a euphemism for a further act of vandalism) was taking place in Princes Street, and there was a huge gap near to Hanover Street, next to the former premises of the Clydesdale Bank.

A handful of enterprising gentlemen from Glasgow decided that the bank had on board more money than was necessary for its own use and that, on an equitable basis, there was no reason why they should not have some of it for themselves. Glasgow has never been short of egalitarians. Despite what some people say to the contrary, in defence of Glasgow I should add that they do considerably outnumber the anarchists.

A plan was hatched. No midday frontal assault with guns blazing in this crowded thoroughfare. A quiet move on a Sunday morning via the adjacent empty space to gain entry while dressed simply as workmen who might be engaged on a next-door site.

In order to rob a bank in this way, however, it is not only necessary to gain entrance to the premises. This in itself will be a waste of time. It is necessary to gain entry to the safe.

This highly-skilled task requires outside assistance—from a top-class specialist. There was no Johnnie Ramensky the Polish cracksman and supreme expert to turn to any more. Johnny, released to be a "help" during the war had returned to his "wicked" ways, used up his ration of goodwill and being in debt once more to society, incarcerated. In Edinburgh, however, there was an acknowledged expert, the master of his craft, believed by the police to be the only free man in Scotland who could perform the vital task.

His name was Hugh Kelly Mannion. He was a gentle man, his skills were known to the police whom he filled with apprehension but to whom he never at any time offered violence. No one now, as I read my papers, could match him. Mannion could have passed unnoticed in a crowd, as he frequently did on a Saturday afternoon at Tynecastle Park while supporting his favourite football team, Heart of Midlothian. To him it was surmised by the police, the gang would have to go for expert assistance in "blowing" the safe.

Sunday came.

Entry to the bank was gained without difficulty, or the raising of suspicion, and inside the gang, whoever they comprised, began in the security of their isolation to plot the next move.

The nasty word "co-incidence" keeps cropping up, however, and fate that day was not on the side of the intruders.

By a hundred to one chance the manager of the bank decided to visit his branch. On the likelihood of his going there on a Sunday you could safely have taken a bet. It would not generally even have been within his contemplation, but there was something which he suddenly decided should have his attention that day. It certainly had nothing to do with the contemplation of a robbery.

At twelve noon he entered by the main door and surprised the uninvited visitors. To-day his body might well have been sprawled on the floor, but these were not murderers. On his arrival they scattered in different directions while he raised the alarm. In no time the police came on the scene, and eventually a number of arrests were made. But if Hugh Kelly Mannion had been in the bank he was certainly not arrested inside or outside the bank. He was picked up later, one suspected, as being the only man capable of doing the main job, i.e. opening the safe.

I was briefed by Freddie Whitelaw WS, who did not often become involved in criminal cases, to defend Hugh Kelly Mannion.

When I read the papers and saw the part alleged to have been played by the others it struck me that one at least (by the name of Fee) must have a very good chance of being acquitted. I mentioned this in passing by way of a tip to young Nicholas Fairbairn, then an eager junior in the hope that his clerk might help him to be involved. He acted for a wide variety of Glasgow Solicitors including those representing each of the co-accused. Nicky was later instructed, gave his usual professional performance and in fact as I had guessed Fee was acquitted— but not his other Glasgow companions.

My concern of course was Hugh Kelly Mannion. He was the prime target for the police. He had been arrested not all that long after the gang had been surprised, but many miles away.

There appeared to be flaws in the police evidence but, when it came to the crunch, they had done their homework in such a way that there was sufficient evidence to entitle a jury to convict, if so minded.

The crucial evidence was that on identification.

Without reliable and credible evidence given clearly that Mannion had been seen in the proximity of the bank at the time of the sudden flight, which struck me on my information that he was unlikely to be, then even if other Crown evidence were to be believed, conviction seemed improbable. There were no amateurish visiting cards such as fingerprints to be produced.

I directed a firm attack on the witness who said he had seen Mannion shortly after twelve o'clock in Rose Street Lane behind the bank, walking away. On my information this allegation was most unlikely to be true.

Where did this evidence come from? Not from the police themselves. I am told that it may be difficult to find a number of police officers in Rose Street on a Saturday night when all sorts of criminal offences are liable to be committed. To find police officers patrolling there on Sunday morning would be highly unlikely.

It would be even more unlikely that any civilian witness, had he been passing by chance in what would have been, on Sunday morning, virtually a deserted area, would have been able to recognise Hugh Kelly Mannion in court, even assuming that he had seen him on that Sunday morning. Mannion as I have said was a man who could melt faceless anywhere. Properly used and trained he might have been a good "spy".

You may wonder then who was the "star" police witness. If not in the police he was certainly "one of the family". The son of a police officer, he just happened, yes happened to be walking in Rose Street by chance on a Sunday morning for no reason that was abundantly clear. Perhaps he just wanted to see what some of the Princes Street shops looked like from the rear, when they were closed. I do not know.

For some reason, however, he said that he knew Hugh Kelly Mannion by sight. Perhaps he was also a Hearts supporter and had stood next to him on the terracing at Tynecastle. The matter was not clear. One thing was clear. He stuck to his guns and no matter what question I put, insisted that he had seen Mannion at the locus. The jury believed him. It is their function to decide.

Mannion received a sentence of eight years' imprisonment.

I do not know if Mannion was there. He himself stoutly denied it. I do know that even now I have a lingering suspicion about part of the evidence which enabled a jury to convict him.

23.

JUDICIAL IGNORANCE

There is always a great move afoot to educate the judiciary in the knowledge of what goes on in the real world.

The popular view of judicial ignorance is exemplified in that delightful cartoon which shows, in the foreground the back of a judge, further beyond him the bench, in the background Counsel, and then distantly the public.

The judge is asking "And what is a pin-up?"

In the forefront of the picture also, beneath the bench, visible to the judge only, and hidden from the public gaze, are depicted a number of young ladies in scant attire.

It is not entirely without substance. In the Scottish Court of Criminal Appeal, appearing on behalf of an Aberdeenshire publican who had been convicted by Sheriff W. R. Walker in Banff Sheriff Court of selling water with too little whisky in it, I had to explain the working of the optic measure—how the bottle was inverted on the gantry and how the precious liquid ran into the glass below when pressure was applied.

Lord Guthrie who had obviously heard of Sir Isaac Newton but was less familiar with Arthur Bell, and who was clearly puzzled by an operation which he had never seen in practice, declared. "but I don't understand how the open bottle can be upside down and the whisky doesn't run out". Lord Clyde chuckled . Perhaps he had just enjoyed his favourite breakfast cereal—Cocopops, he rocked with laughter. At any rate this was in marked contrast to his reaction on the occasion after a Bar Dinner when a Senior Counsel who seldom enjoyed his ear in Court playfully hung a red street lamp on his door-handle.

On another occasion Lord Migdale had difficulty in grasping the concept of a Christmas Club (where people contribute modest sums throughout the year and thus accumulate funds to provide the necessities for the festive season). Having had the good fortune to marry a granddaughter of Andrew Carnegie who sadly died of polio at the age of twenty-nine leaving five children, and to spend his summers at Skibo Castle this particular method of saving would have been an unlikely topic at his dinner table.

A Christmas Club? There was the New Club in Princes Street, there was the golf club of the Honourable Company of Edinburgh Golfers at Muirfield, but they functioned all the year round. A Christmas Club seemed a very short lived affair. His Lordship shook his head in puzzlement. To another who was asked where he met the defender the witness answered "Ah met him in a pub" "What's that" said Lord Migdale who was slightly deaf, "You met him in your club?"

The only club this witness would have recognised would have been an offensive weapon.

Again after leading evidence before Lord Strachan in an 'adultery' case, of how a man had picked up a woman and repaired to bed with her after lunch, I suggested to His Lordship that this was clearly no simulate act of adultery. His Lordship, a Church elder and Procurator of the General Assembly of the Church of Scotland who found it difficult to comprehend that such an activity could take place at that time of the day replied, "It is on that matter that I have the gravest doubt". He would have been astonished if he had heard the late Jim Blackwell, a fellow member of mine in the R & A, relate to me how in India he was once bidden to play in a four at golf with the legendary Walter Hagan. Three of them waited for ages on the tee for the great man to arrive. At last, the story goes, he stumbled out of a rickshaw full of apology, "I'm sorry I'm late gentlemen but I've just been having a matinee with a little woman".

Yet Lord Strachan was a kindly man who had suffered the

privations of war in the trenches where he lost a leg, and the heart felt regret as he told me of not being free to defend a man on a murder charge; the very man who with total disregard for his own life had rescued him from no-man's land.

In furtherance of this process of education however an attractive suggestion was advanced: that those who hand out sentences should visit the environment to which they have committed some of their fellow-citizens and meet some of the inmates. I looked forward to this, for people in prison are not generally without a sense of humour. After all, Peter Craigmyle one of Scotland's best known soccer referees who understood this went to Peterhead Prison with a concert party and exercised his fine singing voice to rapturous applause by rendering "Bless this House" and "Home, Sweet, Home".

On reaching the words "There's no place like home" he was warmly applauded by the inmates. He was merely, of course, anticipating the sentiments of a later prisoner elsewhere who responded to the graffiti call of "Free Nelson Mandela" by chalking up on the wall "F— Nelson Mandela. Free ME".

So, one day, it was arranged that a number of Sheriffs should attend not to amuse, or to be amused, but to be better informed, at the Polmont Institution near Falkirk which housed young offenders. Our party included many who had long judicial experience including Sheriff Dick QC (later Sir John Dick QC Sheriff Principal of Glasgow and Strathkelvin) and Sheriff Ronald Ireland QC (later Sheriff Principal of Grampian). It was agreed that a number of offenders be brought to us in a group, as informally as possible, and for some reason, that I should act as spokesman.

A few sat down at the side, and one in front of me. It was all very relaxed. By prior arrangement I proffered him a cigarette which was freely accepted.

"Tell me", I said, "why are you in here?"

"Car theft" he droned in reply.

"But you wouldn't be here just for taking one car. What else have you been doing?"

"It's aye been car theft".

"Tell me about the last one". Interest anyone in his own theme and he will soon expand.

"Well, ye see", he confided, "I'd just come oot o' hospital and ma feet were fair killin' me, and I just happened to have a bunch of car keys on me, so I took this car."

"Do you realise that our job is to protect the public and to stop people like you from stealing other people's motor-cars?"

"Aye".

"What do you think we'd have to do to stop you stealing cars?"

Before he could think of an answer it came from the wings. Two of his mates awaiting their turn had been sitting silent. On hearing the last question I clearly heard one whisper to the other "Cut his feet aff".

Judges, I suppose, do still have a lot to learn from the public, particularly in regard to sentence.

24.

A STEP UP

I suppose that it will always be a matter of some pride for any practising member of the bar, in my case eleven and a half years—to attain the rank and dignity of Queen's Counsel, and to rustle a new "silk" gown, even if its material content be largely nylon. As a young junior one walked in awe of these superior beings of whom there would only effectively be about twenty-five to thirty in practice in the whole of Scotland.

With more work and more money available to pay them many more lawyers have now gone to the Bar and the number of Queen's Counsel has risen. Many possess a considerable talent but there are some of whom one would not instinctively walk in awe.

The delicate question of whether one would seek to step up would involve initially a confidential discussion with one's clerk to assess whether a successful junior practice was ready to be repeated at a higher level. If he thought so, he would have a private word with the Dean of the Faculty of Advocates. The Dean's approval would lead to a private whisper from him to the Lord President whose approval would be transmitted to the Secretary of State on whose advise the Queen would act. No formal application would be made until the Lord President gave his approval so that in the event of any "no" at that stage the aspiration would be shelved and never become public.

After the Lord President's approval a letter had to be written to every junior advocate senior to the applicant informing him on one's interest. Thus the matter became public, but it was never known of any rejection to be made by that time, to the application. The recent intervention of the Lord Advocate in one case seems unprecedented. Any comment must await developments.

Advocates may be considered for appointment as Queen's Counsel, it is said, after acquiring a large practice, or after moderate practice accompanied by a longer period of time at the Bar; by achieving academic distinction; by appointment to some important office; to preserve a balance in the seniority system, or by propinquity to someone in a high place it is sometimes suggested. The last I doubt.

For most, however, or certainly it used to be, the real "decoration" or elevation in rank had to be earned on the "battlefield", the floor of a Court, and was not one which "came up with the rations". When appointment was made to important office in those days one expected a "silk" to fill it, not as now sometimes for the appointment to be given to a less experienced or unproven junior who has beavered about in "union" or quasi-political activities and then say because it is a high office we have given him we shall have to make this junior a QC.

I understand from some (who have not taken "silk") and no doubt in cases harbour a tinge of envy, that the recipients of "silk" from the "rations" are known cheerfully as "Nylons". When I asked one the reason for this it was explained to me that they were called "Nylons" because they were artificial silks. A reminder of the sharp cutting edge of the lawyer's tongue.

For those who had gained their QC in the field it was an arduous and testing experience to move up. One would then be instructed solely on one's competence, being in charge of the case, in contrast to the many briefs sent to "covering" junior counsel who did not carry the ultimate responsibility and to whom briefs were sometimes sent on a purely social basis. When you take "silk" you virtually empty your whole diary of every court instruction you hold, and wait to see when and how you can fill up the blanks at a higher level.

I make no bones that when I took "silk" I mused to myself that what I wanted immediately, in order that solicitors would be aware of my new status, was a "big" case:— a) criminal preferably, b) sensational, c) well publicised, d) difficult, and e) "Which will last for days, spread my name all over the newspapers finishing up with a triumphant acquittal". Then I woke up.

Hmm. Not much to ask for.

Luckily I got to first base promptly. It was August 1961. A Criminal case arrived. It was to be heard by a Sheriff and jury in Haddington Sheriff Court. My junior was Ian Kirkwood now an extremely able and workaholic judge (Lord Kirkwood). One fly in the ointment already. The poor chap, a most conscientious junior, turned up late and received from me a small "rocket". This was prompted not by new rank but I suppose, strangely, nervousness. The second fly in the ointment was that the case was before Sheriff KWB Middleton.

I never knew the man socially. He may have been kind to children and dumb animals, but, along with Sheriff Charles du bois Murray at Jedburgh, he formed a duo before whom I did not enjoy appearing.

When I used to encounter him in Edinburgh Sheriff Court in summary trial he seemed to wait until I got the answer I wanted from a witness, then pose the question in his own way and write down the answer he got: often to my disadvantage.

When I was addressing him he would suddenly yawn so widely that you could have popped the Sheriff Clerk sitting below into his mouth. (Heavens, I would think to myself I can't be THAT bad). Later, I was relieved to learn that other advocates were treated in the same "open" fashion. It could, on the other hand, be said in Middleton's defence that while the Courts were never short of hot air in one form or another, they were fairly short of oxygen. They still are. We live in a country that does not seem to understand air-conditioning.

The case however also took me to second base very quickly. There were four serious charges of assault against my client. It was a husband and wife scenario: not the run of the mill thump on the earhole by the man, or the propulsion in his direction of the full dinner plate, Daddy Sauce and all, by the wife which in some homes appeared to be regular occurrences, especially when father arrived home late without the pay packet after a flirtation with slow racehorses and quick drinks.

It was mainly a seaside scene, with the husband alleged to have done all manner of things, but mainly having dragged her over the sands to the water, not to make her drink, but to immerse her and thus "cleanse" her of all the black marks which she had accumulated.

It was story book stuff and the press lapped it up. The popular dailies carried it in a middle page spread and no doubt hoped that each morning people would rush to their newsagents to obtain the "next thrilling instalment". The press had not then realised the commercial value of page three, or the mileage to be obtained from the Royal Family, dead princesses or wayward politicians.

Now unfortunately to the difficulties. There was plenty of evidence against my client. There was also Sheriff Middleton who apparently had not changed his habits. As I began my cross-examination he would wait until I had finished and then pop his own question. This time, however, there was a jury and a shorthand writer.

When he suddenly put the most glaring leading question to a man in the box I rose swiftly with all the brief authority of my new senior rank, and more importantly in the knowledge that the jury, not he, would ultimately determine the verdict.

"With respect, My Lord", I said, "I think the answer might come better from the witness". This was no form of respect at all, this was impertinent. It was also effective beyond my wildest dreams. Sheriff Middleton for a moment looked astounded but—he kept his mouth shut. Even better, from then on he continued to keep it shut. He did not even yawn.

When the jury retired, they were some time in reaching their verdict. One cannot predict a verdict from the length of time a jury are out. There are times, however, when one would not have wanted them back too soon.

Eventually they returned.

On all four charges the verdict was exactly the same.

As the question was put to the foreman of the jury, this was before the age of spokespersons, on each charge separately his answer was the same.

The jury by a majority of 10 to 5 find the charge "Not Proven" I could scarcely have asked for anything better. Another senior practice was launched. Other cases soon followed.

25

ASK A SILLY-QUESTION

Lawyers speak often of the necessity when defending to avoid asking superfluous questions. We have all been guilty at times. To go on and on may give an ignorant client the impression that he is getting his money's worth, or, alternatively value for the money provided by the state for his defence. The best fighters are not those whose arms flail all the time.

It can be fatal.

I was sitting with a jury in Glasgow on the trial of two police officers. It was clearly an anxious case, not only for the officers with their whole careers in the balance, but for the two solicitors defending them. They were both keen to impress.

One of those was Leonard Murray one of the abler solicitors in my time to plead in Glasgow Sheriff Court. He would not have disagreed with that opinion. The other was also an experienced practitioner.

From the outset it was obvious that they were going to give the witnesses a hard time. Strangely, for once it looked as if they intended to give myself on the bench a hard time as well.

Such situations I confess never frighten me and are unlikely to yield a dividend for the investor.

True, I have known cases where an inexperienced or insecure judge may be temporarily ruffled by blandishments from below. In general, however, it is bad tactics. In most cases the person on the bench is, or should be, able to cope. That is why he is there. Even if life is made difficult he or she is unlikely to cave in, and it is he, or she, in the end of the day who holds the whiphand. The foolish footballer who argues with the referee would also do well to bear this in mind.

The only court in which the umpire may be subjected freely to ill manners and gratuitous insult is the professional tennis court.

Good advocacy demands that you gain the ear of the bench not that you try to close it up with a wild punch.

In this case we were about to rise for the day and the evidence had come to an end. A submission was made by the second solicitor that the case against his client should be withdrawn from the jury because of lack of corroboration.

I listened to the motion and to the Crown in reply.

I indicated, quoting a certain passage from my own hand-written note, that I considered that there was sufficient evidence to go to the jury.

There was some challenge, however, as to whether the defence accepted that the evidence verbatim, had been precisely as I had noted it.

Time was wearing on. I decided to rise for the day. I indicated to the defence solicitor however that I would hear him again in the morning and in fairness would put before him, by which time it would be available to me, the typed transcription of the relevant part of the evidence as noted by the official short hand writer.

We rose.

On the following morning he was read out the few lines of the evidence which I considered fatal to his submission.

He saw the point. I spared his blushes despite his brusqueness to me the previous day. He is a courteous and able practitioner and everyone makes mistakes. That is why I spare him now by concealing his name.

Few others there—if any—would understand what had transpired. He himself, would be intelligent enough to receive the message.

I, refused his motion and allowed the case against his client to go to the jury. The reason?

In respect of the answer by a witness to a totally unnecessary question put by himself, of all things in re-examination, the little evidence required to afford corroboration of the case against his client was elicited by none other than himself.

How he must have wished that he had kept his big mouth shut.

26.

CANNED GOODS

There is a fairly new form of procedure in the Sheriff Court for small claims. It has been conceived with the best will in the world.

It enables a litigant more readily to present his own case. It may provide a form of cheap and quick justice for those who cannot afford, or do not wish to be involved in the expense and delay of a law-suit. Admirable you may think.

There are, however, difficulties.

Cases have to be heard by a professional judge (in this procedure a Sheriff). With the best will in the world HE cannot disregard the law or throw the rules of evidence and procedure out of the window.

It is not just a case for the judgement of Solomon. It also requires the patience of Job.

The litigant is generally unlikely to know the law, and certainly the rules of evidence and procedure will be a closed book. The disadvantages will be at once obvious. That is perhaps why it used to be said that the man who is his own lawyer has a fool for a client.

Angry, cunning, inarticulate, nervous, obstinate, poor, pig-headed, quiet respectful, all types of people who have a genuine grievance to air, mount and spur on their own chargers, without the benefit of a single riding lesson. Not surprisingly some fall off and others gallop uncontrollably in the wrong direction.

The Bench as I have said must exercise infinite patience. At the end of the day they all have to be rounded up.

Mr Liquat Ali Khan (not his real name) like many of his countrymen had a high regard for money. To accumulate it was paramount. To part with it was to declare a brief period of mourning.

Thus he came before me to present his own case. Although it was not his native tongue he had no difficulty with the English language. It is most important for the Bench to ascertain at the outset from those of a different ethnic origin whether they have difficulties with the English language.

Mr "Ali" had clearly read the appropriate Act of Parliament with more care than some of the young solicitors who cut their teeth in minor cases. In cross examination he asked many relevant questions.

When time came for him to give his own evidence he was lucid and voluble. Then, however, he became subject to cross examination.

The wind now changed and blew in a different direction.

As with many from overseas when faced with an awkward question he began to discover some difficulty with the English language.

When other embarrassing questions were posed, his understanding and his memory seemed to have deserted him.

At last, faced with a perfectly simple question he withdrew, and relapsed when the question was repeated, into total silence.

"Come, Mr Ali", I urged him gently, "You seem to be quite an intelligent man, The question is quite straightforward. Would you please answer it".

"My Lord", he replied "You say that I am a highly intelligent man. I am not a clever man. I am just a small shop-keeper who sells tins of beans".

"Well Mr Ali", I said to him pointedly, "You know how many beans make five".

He understood at once the English idiom and the censure implied in my comment. He answered the question, but in doing so unfortunately lost his case.

27.

LET NO MAN PUT ASUNDER

In the House of Lords case of *Hyde* v *Hyde* in 1863, a judge described marriage as "the union of one man and one woman for life to the exclusion of all others"

Four marriages in ten now end in divorce and a number of others would not fall within the 1863 definition. Had society, or some of it, not accepted that close relationships, lasting or transitory, may be carried on without general censure outside the bond of marriage, the proportion of divorces would be higher.

In this context the words of Dame Maud Royden who carried on a deep, unconsummated relationship for many years with a married man strike an add chord when she exclaimed to him passionately " To think that tonight the meanest peasant in the land can have what we can never have".

Although there were far fewer divorces, by 1959 I had already done a thousand of them. By 1965 when I had stopped counting I had the largest Q.C.'s divorce practice in Scotland. Curious, pathetic or humorous commentaries on human relationship. Modern partners are often less thick-skinned. One should not be surprised to hear for example of the divorce case of *Jekyll* v *Jekyll* as well as *Hyde* v *Hyde*. They were not of course cross-actions. Mr Jekyll had not gone off with Mrs Hyde, or vice versa.

An occasional glance at the divorce lists used to throw up some interesting combinations.

On the Court of Session rolls, for example, I have warmed to the pairing of contestants such as *Darling* v *Darling*, *Joyner* v *Joyner*, *Kean* v *Kean* and *Love* v *Love* which have seemed less appropriate than *Spouse* v *Spouse* or *Splitt* v *Splitt* which seemed apt.

On another occasion I have noticed *Husband* v *Husband*. The husband of course was not a wife, but the wife was a Husband.

Imagine my concern, however, one day in being briefed for one of the parties in the case of *Wedlock* v *Wedlock*.

Needless to say, it ended successfully—in divorce.

28.

PROTECTING A GENTLEMAN

Rape once more. The High Court in Edinburgh. When I had read the papers sent to me by Alan Finlayson a pleasant humorous outgoing and optimistic Edinburgh solicitor of Messrs Rankin and Reid, SSC, (later to carve a successful career for himself in the field of Social Work and to act as a temporary Sheriff) my reaction was to say to him:— "Is this man pleading guilty? It looked that bad. "Not on your life" beamed Finlayson (a typical Finlayson expression). When I saw my client Mooney (name fictitious) in Saughton Prison he denied rape and confirmed that he would fight the whole distance.

I consoled myself that it is not always the cases that appear blackest at the outset which turn out to be the worst. On the information before me this one certainly did not look promising. In addition, the Crown case was in the hands of the Solicitor-General Ewan Stewart QC (later Lord Stewart) one of the most astute criminal lawyers of my generation. "Penguin" Stewart a "gutsy" little man who won an M.C. with the Royal Scots but who showed more fear on the golf-course.

The jury was empanelled. Amongst their number was a lady whom I had known for some time. Innocently, I hasten to add. It is always pleasant to see a familiar face on the jury. It is of course no guarantee that over the period of the trial one is necessarily looking at a friend.

The case proceeded.

The allegation against Mooney was simple. He had returned to the home of his ex-wife, and gained entry by climbing through the window.

He was not welcome but, nevertheless, she was, if not the target of his everlasting affection, the target of his immediate desire. When she was disposed to resist his advances it was said, he acted promptly.

The Crown case was that, after reducing her to the prone position with her back against the floor, he grasped a standard lamp. It had a long flex. Wrapping the flex round her neck he held her in a helpless position while he lay on top of her with the flex held firmly down at either side of her head. She had little choice it was said in what was to follow. With some temporary adjustment he manipulated himself into a position where, against her will, he proceeded to have sexual relations with her. That if not a matter of fact was the assertion.

The defence of course in such cases is either that penetration was not effected, or if it had been, that the woman had consented. In this case the latter prevailed. It was not of course suggested that she had consented to having her neck encased and constricted in flex.

The woman gave her evidence. I must confess that, as distinct from many such cases, it did not sound totally unconvincing. There was also evidence of marks on her neck. Ominous? On the other hand she did not appear as a particularly sympathetic figure.

One will never learn entirely how to treat a jury, or however perceptive, or bewildered they may be, to know what is passing through the minds of those fifteen people. There is also the added complication that one jury, like the individuals who comprise it, will differ from another.

I have often thought how interesting it would be if one could have four separate juries sitting in a square round the accused, witnesses and counsel, each hearing the same case and receiving the same charge from the judge, and then being sent on their separate ways to return a verdict. Would their verdicts be identical—unlikely. Would they be very similar? Who knows. One will never have the opportunity of finding out.

It used to be said for example, in the days of capital murder that a jury in Perth would not hesitate from bringing in a guilty verdict in a murder case, but that a jury in Dundee would shrink from it. I never defended in a murder case in Perth, but I do remember that when I defended Billy Stark, a well-known Scottish international boxer on a murder charge in Dundee he was found NOT guilty: as indeed were others.

The jury retired to consider the evidence in the case against Mooney. I had no idea what they might do, but I would not have rushed to Ladbrokes had they then been in legitimate business, to put a bet on my client.

It was 12–3 for Not Guilty.

When I left a Court in such cases, after the "hubbub" that follows success, my mind often dwelled not on the moment of "triumph" but on cases where it might have been different. Putting it in such terms, even in Liverpool where I have been generously entertained and spent so much time watching what is still the most successful soccer side that Britain has ever produced they would tell you that you do not always win. This of course every Counsel knows from his own experience, and Liverpool in recent years have found out as other clubs flood their grounds with international circuses whose allegiance has no relevance to the clubs history or tradition but only to its "gold reserves".

One wants to win. That is the object of the game. But how often have I left a Court, win or lose—in a criminal trial there is no draw—wondering where the truth really lay. To that I now turn to the civil court and the divorce case of *Brown* v *Brown.*

Before doing so I should add as a footnote that I happened later to bump into the lady juror whom I knew. I was curious to know what had tilted the balance in my favour. She declined to give a serious answer and replied flippantly that some of the women on the jury had wondered what the woman was complaining about.

29.

DIVORCE—BROWN STUDY

There is nothing spectacular, no obvious headlines, in a divorce case called *Brown* v *Brown*. A common name in Scotland. In fact my maternal grandmother was a Brown. Back at sixteen for holidays from her boarding school she met my grandfather a handsome man some fourteen years her senior, who in no time proposed marriage. Marriage she decided would be better than going back to a girls' boarding school, which not too many Scots girls of that generation would have known. She married at sixteen and at the age of eighty three told me that she had never met a man whom she would rather have married. Perhaps she was lucky. For that Brown, no divorce.

Incidentally, in these days of retreat for the adherents of Sir Walter Raleigh's import, the weed-tobacco, I also recall that at eighty three she confided that what she missed most in the house when my grandfather died, was the aroma of a good cigar. I suppose that, but for passive smoking she might have lived longer.

The case of *Brown* v *Brown* had no family and no tobacco connections. Its only significance lies in its illustration that, in court, a case may be thoroughly spoken to in evidence, debated upon thereafter, adjudicated upon the facts elicited by a competent judge, and yet when it is all over, the question where the truth really lay may never have been touched on. I wonder if it was in this case.

You will find the case reported in 1954 *Scots Law Times*. Since this is not written for the benefit of lawyers, many of whom spend years pouring over law reports, some hacking away at wood without ever seeing the trees, I shall not dwell on the legal report which is there for any of them to read.

This was an undefended action of divorce. Marriage in those

days being regarded as a matter of some consequence, questions of status could only be determined in the Court of Session, as the supreme Civil Court in Scotland. Even to win an undefended divorce could be a real battle. Now when I have sat, of a morning and signed interlocutors granting decree of divorce to twelve people in the space of as many minutes, I occasionally shudder. Marriage (I shall not quote again *Hyde* v *Hyde* in 1863), is not the "in" thing for a large part of the population, but to a large degree it was still in the fifties. Perhaps marriage should be made more difficult or divorces made easier —for example on payment of a small fee at the Post Office, I am not proposing this, but, at that time, divorce could certainly be difficult to obtain.

Brown v *Brown* was not a case for young juniors who then generally cut their teeth on quick adultery—in the Courts I hasten to add in those days, nor was it a chance for a few guineas to be made quickly. For senior juniors the undefended divorces which reached us were only the "headaches" the awkward ones which commanded no higher fees that the "easy" ones. Three guineas was the fee for an undefended proof when I was called to the Bar: that is, unless it was marked "poor" in which case you did it for nothing—except of course for experience which does not buy a case of good claret. This one reached me through the unavailability, if I recollect correctly, of another more senior junior, by name Lionel Daiches (now QC and doyen of the Bar). Why Lionel suddenly became unavailable for *Brown* v *Brown* I do not know, but through the good offices of Messrs Furst and Furst SSC I was asked to take it over at short notice. Twenty minutes.

It was clearly a "stinker". Lionel no doubt had a more difficult problem on his mind.

It was not helped by the fact that the judge was Lord Wheatley who, as a Roman Catholic, was not disposed to reach any height of affability when presiding in a divorce court.

I led evidence on behalf of the husband. It appeared that he was "willing to adhere to his wife" for a period of three years after their separation. This was then a necessary prerequisite for divorce on the ground of desertion. The evidence did little to suggest that the great love of his life had fled him leaving him pining to a shadow for her loss, nor did his behaviour suggest that he was a desirable partner.

It went on and on. Undefended. There was no contradiction, but of course there was Lord Wheatley who applied his thorough professionalism to the whole matter, but gave the clear impression that he would not have welcomed the pursuer as a partner for his next round of golf at Muirfield or his companion in the stand at Hampden Park. He and I exchanged differing views on the acceptability of some of the evidence and the inferences to be drawn from it.

To my infinite relief Lord Wheatley whom, despite his many strictures, I regarded as a fair man eventually in a written judgement granted decree of divorce.

When it was all over, I still had reservations about the whole case.

If you want to know what the law says, it is there in black and white in the official reports'; it is there for posterity. Yes. He was willing to adhere and she was bound to adhere but had not done so. Accordingly, she was in desertion :— Read *Brown* v *Brown* in 1954 *Scots Law Times*.

If you want to know what Herbert Furst SSC my instructing solicitor said to me after the case it was this:—

"You know Mr Bell, I don't think that he *really* wanted to live with her. The trouble I understand was that when they went to bed at night, he couldn't stand the smell from her private parts".

When, if ever, do we know in the law where the real truth lies?

30.

GAME, SET AND NO MATCH

The landlord of the Brown Cow public house a well known West of Scotland hostelry (the colour was not brown and the animal was not a cow—I use the name only as a camouflage) was ill at ease in his matrimonial relationship. His preference was for the cellar rather than the boudoir. The pleasure with which he was wont to patronise generously the stock on his own premises was not echoed in the attention which he lavished in his relationship with his partner in marriage.

Meanwhile his wife who had different priorities, not that she particularly wanted him in the boudoir, just that she wanted him out of the cellar, had also decided that something should be done about it.

So it came about that I was instructed on her behalf to seek every available remedy; decree of divorce, aliment for her, custody of and aliment for the children, and of course the expenses of the action. The evidence was overwhelming.

When served with the writ, however the landlord was none too pleased. It was an affront to his pride and a threat to his pocket. He immediately instructed defences to be lodged and battle was joined in which he stubbornly resisted every claim on him. It went on for four days and despite a brave but forlorn fight by his Senior Counsel, R.A. Bennett Q.C., he went straight down the drain. He could scarcely have engineered his downfall better. He lost on every count

Yet when it was all over he must, apart from the financial implications, have taken some satisfaction from the nature in which he had got rid of his menage. Outside of the bar, perhaps, he was clearly not a man for half measures.

At four o'clock on a bitter February morning with the snow

lying thick on the ground he ejected his screaming wife, his wailing children and, yes, his terrified mother-in-law at the point of a shotgun into the frozen darkness and locked the door firmly behind them.

This gesture of theatrical finality while affording temporary relief was clearly unwise and thus should not commend itself to other husbands who may have read the last paragraph with envy or interest, and may have had at times the inclination to carry out a similar exercise.

In the present age of sexual equality I should of course add that such action would also be available to a wife.

31.

UP FOR THE CUP

The judge, the jury and the public might be surprised if they knew of some of the little asides that take place in Court even on the most solemn occasions.

It was Wednesday, the third day of another murder trial, this one in the High Court in Edinburgh. The public galleries were packed as if the Beatles were about to come on. Upstairs and downstairs were full. On one side of the Court sat the jury, on the other a number of unoccupied counsel who were listening. The press were there in strength.

At that time, having already declined an invitation from Harry Swan, the Chairman, an ex-President of the Scottish Football Association to join the Board of Hibernian Football Club, I bore the cheerful burden of being a director of Heart of Midlothian Football Club. Even this I only did after consultation with the Dean of Faculty of Advocates. Had he advised against it I would have declined. No Queens Counsel to my knowledge had previously joined the Board of a Soccer Club.

Brian Appleby Q.C. with Nottingham Forest (now a Circuit Judge in England) and Donald Findlay Q.C. with Rangers have since followed along the same trail. I do not suppose that anyone confronted with a similar offer to-day would stop to ask.

In those days Hearts had something to cheer about. Wednesday was not just the third day of a murder trial, it was the day on which the draw would be make for the next round of the Scottish Cup in which Hearts were involved. I was anxious to know who our opponents would be.

Waiting until the Crown led a brief formal witness, when any necessary questions could be asked by my junior, I left the Court and shot to the telephone. There was a private number which I could use to phone Tynecastle Park. No luck. No news yet. I returned to court, leaving instructions that news of the draw should be passed as soon as possible.

Ten minutes later a side door of the court opened and a court official moved swiftly in my direction. He was, visibly to all, clutching a sheet of white paper. He came gingerly forward to the table where I was sitting and passed it over. I looked at it, thanked him, nodded gravely, and he departed.

The whole courtroom peered at this paper and whisperers wondered what dramatic development was about to take place in the murder case. We were not in the jurisdictions of Perry Mason or O.J. Simpson. What was this vital piece of information which had been brought to my attention?

I can tell them all now.

On the paper placed before me was written simply four words:—

"Rangers or Dundee (away)".

As an irrelevant sequel it was, in the event, Rangers we had to play. A 1–1 draw at Ibrox on Saturday meant a replay in Edinburgh on a Wednesday. In those days I used to promise to buy someone dinner if Hearts or Hibernian ever played Rangers or Celtic with a referee who hailed from Edinburgh. To have a Glasgow or West of Scotland referee on such occasions was commonplace, on one occasion even to have the referee address Heart players by their surnames and Rangers players by their Christian names. On Tuesday someone rushed to tell me that, for the replay on Wednesday the original referee was injured and his place would be taken by an Edinburgh referee. This was thought—wrongly of course—to give the Edinburgh side a better chance of winning or at least a lesser likelihood of losing. "Edinburgh referee?" I asked disbelievingly. "Yes, W J Mullen of Dalkeith". I wriggled "Dalkeith is not Edinburgh".

Mullen it was. Four minutes from time Donald Ford the Hearts centre-forward slipped the ball neatly through the legs of Eric Sorensen the Rangers Danish goalkeeper and Hearts won 1–0. Nothing to do with the referee.

Sadly, later, they lost in the final 3–1 to Dunfermline Athletic. Nevertheless the Hearts players like the accused in the murder case escaped hanging. It had of course by then been abolished.

32.

A TALE FROM TWO CITIES

At the height of the "cold war" it was not common in Edinburgh to pass the time of day with a Russian intellectual and particularly to speak to one anywhere outwith earshot of an attentive fellow countryman. It was accordingly a double bonus for one or two busy members of the Scottish Bar to be able to persuade a distinguished professor of law from Moscow to join us on his own for a drink and to tell us a little bit about how justice operated at home.

We chatted over a number of preliminary topics. Naturally the transparent odourless spirit which finds little favour with my generation, vodka, and the way to drink it were discussed. Now of course many of our own youth, anxious to acquire the temporary "lift" from consuming alcohol, drown it in orange juice, blackcurrant and God knows what, while their ignorant elders enjoy the subtle flavour of a good malt whisky. The Russian I observed was not averse to Scotch whisky although he did not down it in one smartly and exhale the fumes quickly as I have heard recommended for vodka. Perhaps we were too slow for him.

We were of course anxious to hear a little of the operation of justice in the Soviet Union and the subject was soon raised. No one was impolite enough to mention the names of Stalin or even Beria in this context, nor did our new comrade feel obliged to rest his case for Russian justice on his great leader. Our guest however, did pull back the curtain slightly to disclose the merest shaft of enlightenment. I suspect this was due to the tongue in his cheek, rather than the whisky in his body. He had a hard head.

His anecdote drew strength from the courts in Moscow

before the Revolution. I refer to the one in 1917. There was, he said, an eminent counsel who was asked to defend in what appeared to be a very trivial case for the great man. His services were sought to defend a priest on a charge of stealing a pig. Clearly both justice and religion were high in the priorities of pre-Revolutionary Russian society.

His friends urged him to allow the defence to be dealt with by some lesser light. It would do nothing for his reputation they urged, or are alleged to have urged. Counsel, however, was adamant. He would defend this man.

The trial proceeded before a jury. The prosecutor led witness after witness in support of the charge. No matter what the evidence, counsel declined the opportunity to challenge by cross-examination what the witness had said. Everyone in Court was mystified or perplexed that evidence, however damaging, appeared to be allowed to go undisputed. No evidence was led for the defence.

At the end of the evidence the prosecutor addressed the jury and suggested that his own case was overwhelming. It had clearly been established that the priest had stolen the pig. There was no evidence to the contrary. The priest must be found guilty.

The eminent Moscow counsel for the first time roused himself to address the jury. He was totally unflummoxed. His plea to the jury was short and to the point.

" Members of the jury" he boomed, pointing to his client "Many a time this man has forgiven you your sins. To-day I ask you to forgive him his".

The jury acquitted the priest.

We could not of course match this, nor as practitioners risk putting it to the test. It would have been interesting however had he come back years later to hear how we administer justice in Scotland.

As Bulganin and Kruschov the Russian leaders marched through the streets of Edinburgh in procession and in company with George Pottinger, then a senior civil servant it was said that, a distance away, some high-spirited students let off a load of fireworks to mark the occasion. One of the Russians, clearly in alarm, turned and said "What is that?"

As they all walked on with dead pan faces Pottinger is alleged to have replied solemnly "Gunfire".

The anxious Russian was quick to respond. "Will there be many dead?"

Pottinger still walking with grave countenance is stated to have whispered confidentially "Only a few".

33.

BUS RIDE

There are different ways I am told of skinning a cat.

This may well have been known to the woman in Newcastle who received a six months' prison sentence it is reported, after selling for human consumption some unfortunate dead pussies —without their outer covering—under the inviting label of "Scotch hares". The choice is often neglected in the resolution of legal problems but may be the subject of debate in a new Scottish Parliament.

I give but one example from a totally different field of law. Far removed—at least I hope so—from the criminal courts, and to do with omnibuses rather than cats. I refer to the Road Traffic Commissioners.

The country (Great Britain) for administrative purposes was divided into eleven regions, Scotland constituting one, each presided over by a Commissioner who was generally a lawyer but who had wide legal powers—particularly, for example, as in the case to which I now refer, with applications for a new omnibus route. This was long before the Conservative party decided to open the whole matter up to various allegedly competing interests and the name Stagecoach was more readily associated with Wells Fargo.

In the fifties, as now, the franchise to run a bus service, and more particularly to obtain a new one, could be a lucrative business for the operator. This was recognised by a number of enterprising business men, but to obtain a new one, application of course was necessary, and seldom granted. It was a time when private enterprise was viewed with grave suspicion.

The Commissioner in Scotland was a Mr William Quinn who had previous associations with the Labour party and who had obtained his appointment when that party was, if I may say, in the driving seat.

I was instructed by a firm of solicitors, then known as McRobert, Son and Hutchison, a well known and respected business, to appear before Mr. Quinn in an application for a bus operator in Lanarkshire, who wished to obtain a licence for a new route in the Auchengeoch area—a mining district which sadly at one time was the scene of a pit disaster involving considerable loss of life.

When I looked at the papers I almost said "Forget it, you are wasting you time". When I looked more closely, however, I thought that, while not optimistic, it was at least worth a shot.

The reason why I originally thought it to be hopeless was that an application had been turned down for the same man, for the same route, by the same Commissioner a mere six weeks before.

The reason why I altered my opinion was that on looking at the history of the previous application I could see that, whatever might have transpired at the hearing, and whatever the merits, it had failed simply for lack of presentation.

A young, inexperienced solicitor had been entrusted with the case. In fairness to him he had not put forward the best evidence to back the application, and had not made out the real strength of the case. The Commissioner really had had no option but to refuse the application. It was time as my friends in South Africa would say "to make a plan". In Scotland to decide how to skin the cat.

It struck me that it was important to find out the strength of local opinion on both the desirability, and the necessity, of such a route. It would obviously be important in addition to know what local people of some standing thought. Especially local people whose views might carry some weight.

Lawyers do not themselves make all the bullets they fire. They must, however, be able to recognise the best people who make them, and to seek to fire them to advantage.

I happened to know—the cat is now in trouble—that Mr Quinn was a close friend of Miss Margaret Herbison, the local Member of Parliament for North Lanarkshire, an able and influential politician who had the welfare of her constituents at heart. The area must breed them, for they have had since in the area closeby outstanding Labour members such as the late John Smith QC., the former Leader of her Majesty's Opposition, whom many of us knew and Tom Clark *inter alia* a Shadow Secretary of State for Scotland.

It occurred to me that it would be a good idea to find out what Miss Herbison's views were on the matter. Mr Quinn might not share them, but on the other hand he would certainly listen carefully as we all do, to the views of an old and respected friend. I discovered that Miss Herbison's views were favourable. A Member of Parliament is generally pleased to help a constituent.

So at the hearing I concentrated less on the usual weapons in a lawyer's armoury. I do not know what impression such other evidence as I led, made on Mr Quinn, but the cat was now approaching surgery.

I brought out the biggest cutting instrument in my armoury, namely a letter which I had obtained, written by no less a person than the redoubtable Miss Herbison. It was long and lucid, and much in favour of the venture. I read it to Mr Quinn slowly, and with emphasis on the friendliest parts. He listened with care. I do not know whether it had any influence on the result. I suspect that it may have had some bearing, Miss Herbison certainly proved a very good "counsel".

Mr Quinn granted the application.

Some time later my client, I am told, sold out to considerable financial advantage. Not of course to mine.

34.

DOCTOR IN TROUBLE

I do not suppose that you visit on a regular basis the imposing headquarters of the General Medical Council in Wimpole Street London W1, or attend the hearings of its disciplinary body who listen to complaints against members of the medical profession. They are kept busy.

Robert Rose, a general medical practitioner whom I had been asked to represent, was not my first client to be called to account there. The previous one the Airdrie doctor for whom I had acted as junior counsel in a preceding criminal prosecution which brought him into conflict with his own professional disciplinary body, had thought it sufficient to instruct only my senior, John Wheatley QC (later Lord Wheatley). A prudent economy.

Now was the time to see the place at first hand.

It seemed desirable to wear, of course, standard professional garb.

So when a taxi deposited me at the front door I emerged bowler-hatted in black jacket and striped trousers with a rolled umbrella and briefcase. The briefcase did not contain, as was alleged of so many young London businessmen at that time, who dressed smartly to keep up appearance, my lunch-time sandwiches, but the type of dress was certainly familiar to the uniformed commissionaire who greeted me and directed me.

He must have misheard what I said, and I assumed that the room to which I was being conducted was the one set aside for the use of counsel. When I found myself amongst a group of other men similarly attired I did not even raise an eye-brow. I sat down to await my client and my instructing solicitor.

It was only when snatches of conversation between some of those present began to penetrate that I realised that I was in the wrong company. Very wrong by the sound of it. I was amongst the medical men due to answer complaints against them.

When one said to another "What are you here for?" the question was directed to a tall Ibo with glistening ebony skin "Ah-bortion" he boomed without hesitation or embarrassment in a voice so deep that it might have come up from Paul Robeson's boots and been heard back in the speaker's native eastern Nigeria.

A middle aged, slightly rotund fellow was prancing about chattering like a magpie. His face was pallid and flabby, and his thick lips moist. When someone was rude enough to interrupt him, and to enquire the reason for his presence he dismissed the matter airily and with a nonchalant wave of the hand.

"Act of gross indecency with another male person" he lisped quickly as if this were an everyday occurrence.

Perhaps it was.

My client too, unfortunately, was there because of abortion; the fact was that earlier, in the High Court, on my advice he had admitted to carrying out two illegal abortions. The medical authorities as well as the High Court look coldly on such activities.

I do not know what the collective word is—a rush, a splatter, but there were a number of such cases to be dealt with that day.

Lord Cohen of Birkenhead who presided was courtesy itself. I did my best. In the end of the day, however, there was no way out (perhaps not the best expression to use in such circumstances).

Despite my earnest plea, Rose was struck off. What happened to the Ibo, or to Him-of-the-thick-moist-lips I do not know. Rose I am happy to say was later restored and, in a different area, able to return to a quiet orthodox general practice.

35.

UNDERSTANDING

The defence solicitor appearing in a summary criminal complaint was humming and hawing and wittering on without getting to the point. In Scotland's busiest court it was not welcome.

I had a long day in front of me and was anxious that he should proceed.

His problem was that he was undecided about the relevancy of the charge against his client. In other words, whether the wording of the charge if established in fact was sufficient to instruct a breach of the law by his client.

"I'm not certain whether I understand this charge" he went on.

We all waited with increasing irritation.

"On second thoughts" he said, "I don't"

He was also seeking to tease the Procurator-Fiscal and to show up his department in a poor light for bad draftsmanship.

We all waited.

"On the other hand, my Lord, I think that I can just understand the charge'"

I was beginning to run out of patience.

"Yes, I do understand", he said.

It was time to relieve gently my pent-up feelings.

"That, Mr Jones", I replied, "may reflect great credit on the draftsman". The defence solicitor took the point.

We all remained silent and the case proceeded.

36.

LOVE BITES

I do not know if any Scottish counsel has been there since, but when I appeared in London in front of the General Dental Council's disciplinary body on behalf of a Scottish dentist I was told that I was the first member of the Scottish Bar to do so.

It was a simple and perhaps cheaper matter in such cases to instruct a member of the English Bar who was close at hand.

My client, however was Scottish and had insisted on being represented by Scottish counsel and although I was not a friend, he had asked specifically for myself. Ever since I had kept his secret from everyone when he was sheltering in his St Andrews home Nurse Brennan from Leicester while the nation's press hunted high and low without success to find the girl who was about to marry the Earl of Strathmore he had trusted me.

Amongst the adjudicating body as its legal adviser, the person to "get through to" was Bill Sime (a good friend of mine). We had much in common: W A Sime QC (later Judge Sime) had defended one of the "Great Train Robbers" while at the Bar. He had taken time to get a cricket Blue at Oxford and in 1948 captained Notts in the County Cricket Championship. Later he served the country in both Cyprus and, along with myself, in Northern Ireland. In Cyprus he did not hesitate to take the place of someone shot dead by EOKA, the Greek terrorist organisation. He kept a letter which he received from them a few weeks before leaving Cyprus finally informing him that he could relax as they no longer intended to kill him. This of course was not a signal to relax his guard. Sadly he died within a few weeks of being appointed President of the Forty Club, one of the most prestigious of cricket clubs, but of course many years after he left Cyprus, and unconnected with EOKA.

To return to the Scottish dentist. He was not accused of interfering with a patient under anaesthetic, failing to drill teeth properly or of pulling out the wrong ones. It was alleged however that he had become so obsessed with a young lady patient who did not welcome his advances that he wrote to her, telephoned her, followed her and generally caused her, it was alleged, great distress. In fact it was alleged that he pestered her to the point of distraction.

Sime, as a lawyer lapped it all up. My client appeared to have been less of a danger than E.O.K.A., but when questions began to be asked, however, I could see that I was on a very difficult wicket. In fact I began to feel as if I were in the dentist's chair. The evidence as it emerged seemed greatly at variance with the information in my possession. The paramount consideration for myself suddenly became not the necessity to dismiss all the allegations as hysterical nonsense, but to ensure that my client was free to carry on his practice—a doubt which was growing in my mind.

Counsel must constantly adapt tactically to the changing battlefront.

I thought it prudent suddenly to have a brief word with the English counsel appearing for the General Dental Council. A deal had obviously to be done.

His name was Geoffrey Howe. You may have heard of him. He was highly thought of as Counsel and then still a junior on the fringe of "silk" and about to take the first step towards high office. We asked for an adjournment. The matter was then diplomatically resolved without any penalty, or censure on my client or danger to his practice which at one time seemed certain, when he agreed to give a limited undertaking. It was in the light of the evidence an unavoidable concession. He was thus able to continue his practice and to suffer no penalty.

The work having been done I accepted an invitation to have

a gin and tonic with Geoffrey Howe while we waited for the outcome. A benign-looking fellow, he kindly invited me to luncheon. It was just before his appointment to be QC and then Solicitor-General in England. I told him, in what seems retrospectively an off-hand manner, that I had an urgent meeting that evening in Edinburgh and must turn down his invitation and get back immediately, which I did.

One would not readily turn down an invitation to luncheon from a Chancellor of the Exchequer, or a Deputy Prime Minister, but of course he had not then reached these heights and gave no hint of the "savagery" later attributed to him by Denis Healy.

37.

FOOTSORE

I sat on the Bench on a dull morning, hoping for some light relief. I was not disappointed.

The opening of the Crown case in a summary criminal trial was accompanied by the heavy tread of the first police constable as he marched purposefully towards the witness-box.

As he reached it, the Court Officer announced his presence in ringing terms—"Police Constable William CORNES, my Lord".

"Mm", I thought to myself behind the controlled dead-pan judicial expression, "I suppose you came here on foot".

When P.C. CORNES had completed his evidence he clumped off without any hint that he was making for the nearest chiropodist.

As the next Crown witness stamped in the Court Officer re-exercised his vocal chords. I could hardly believe it.

"Police Sergeant Thomas BUNNION" he boomed.

When he disappeared I waited anxiously. No, we did not have Police Inspector VERUCCA.

38

BULL POINT

Sir Robert Spencer-Nairn, Bt, sold a bull to an eighty-eight year old farmer in Forfar. Such transactions are common in the agricultural world.

It was not the intention of the purchaser that the bull should graze idly in some Angus field, but that it should put itself about in the fulfilment of its own desires, not only to provide some happiness for the farmer's cows, but to provide some pleasure for the farmer himself by increasing his stock.

According to the farmer, however, the bull had failed lamentably—not a single beast in calf. He wanted his money back. Sir Robert's advisers held a contrary view of the bull's capabilities, and having rejected any suggestion of taking back the bull, or indeed of returning the purchase price, the farmer with the characteristic fiery determination of his kind, decided to sue.

The forum was Kirkcaldy Sheriff Court, and soon battle was joined, a vitriolic encounter in which the overlay of a furious antipathy between rival local solicitors on either side rendered even the leading of evidence a difficult matter for the Sheriff to control.

The Hon. Douglas Watson, a partner in Messrs. Fraser, Stoddart and Ballingall WS, Edinburgh (whose father and grandfather incidentally, had been House of Lords judges— Lord Thankerton and Lord Watson respectively, and whose brother was the Hon. David Watson Q.C., for whom I once acted on an unfortunate occasion when his car collided with a bus in Princes Street, asked whether I would mind acting for Sir Robert in a case which had already begun. I accepted.

When I reached Kirkcaldy the temperature had dropped,

but there was of course still the anxious question to be addressed of the bull's capacity to perform the function for which it had been purchased.

The Sheriff, Gerald Paisley Sinclair Shaw, Q.C., was not ill-disposed towards myself. We had been neighbours in Northumberland Street until 1955 before I moved to Heriot Row and handed over there to the future Lord Wylie who sold on to John Douglas of Scotland and Lion's rugby fame, the man who led in Rubstic as winner of the Grand National. In fact Sinclair Shaw when Advocate-Depute in the post-war Labour government had kindly invited me to be his junior in a High Court rape case—for a shilling of reward of course, but of no political significance .

Sinclair Shaw Q.C. (whose original name, unknown to many was Gerald Paisley Jones and who had assumed the name Shaw in deference to his hero George Bernard Shaw) in fact was not happy with his lot in Kirkcaldy. As an ex-chairman of the Scottish Labour Party he had hoped to be made a judge and had even turned down an offer to be made Sheriff Principal of the Lothians as insufficient reward for his services and his abilities. His eventual acceptance of Sheriff in Kirkcaldy he did not regard as fulfilment.

While his reception of myself was pleasant, as no doubt it was to his charming French wife Denise whose courage as a member of the wartime French resistance gained the respect of many of us, he appeared less well-disposed to baronets and bulls.

Evidence was led of some defect in one of the bull's legs which it was said hampered its mobility, and further doubts were cast on its ability to produce seminal fluid, without which the most eager cow could never experience the joys of motherhood.

This latter defect in the bull however was hotly disputed

and so it was decided to put the bull to the test. Not of course in the courtroom which might have been awkward.

Professor Jennings of the West of Scotland Agricultural was brought into the act as an expert—not literally—but under his aegis it was arranged that the bull would be put through its paces.

So, in front of a large audience of agricultural students in a different arena an artificial vagina was rigged up and the bull brought in to confront it.

The result was quite startling. The bull, having made swift contact with the contraption, immediately covered itself in a blaze of glory, and even caused one or two of the audience instinctively to duck.

One student who was in the firing line is alleged to have remarked that it was the youngest piece of veal he had ever tasted.

Thus to an extent the bull was able to emphasise his masculinity, and as an irrelevant sequel Sheriff Sinclair Q.C., was able to underline his own prowess—when the Labour party again came to power—by being promoted to Sheriff Principal of the Lothians the appointment which he had long previously rejected if not the one to which he had originally aspired.

39.

JIMMY BOYLE

You may have heard of Jimmy Boyle.

If you have not, that would not be the fault of a lot of people. In recent years he has not only published two autobiographical volumes "A Sense of Freedom" and "Pain of Confinement", but has also become a media man. He has written, painted and provided psychiatrists and prison reformers with endless scope for debate.

Next year it is said will see the publication of his first novel "Hero of the Underworld!".

At the time with which I deal he was simply classed as one of the detested "hard" men of the Glasgow underworld. Vicious, brutal and dishonest, according to some, particularly the police, his convictions were numerous, and it was said that no one tangled with Jimmy Boyle unless at his peril. Many had lived to vouch for that. Whether all, I do not know. This of course may have nothing to do with his professed love of and residence in Edinburgh where he has recently been invited to join the Lord Provost's committee on Social Exclusion.

William Dunlop, then of Dunlop Daly & Co, one of Glasgow's leading criminal practitioners the father of Sheriff William Dunlop engaged me to appear in Boyle's defence. You will not be surprised when I reveal that it was a murder case. Nor, I should add, Boyle's first appearance on such a charge.

Four sat in the dock, none of them shrinking violets—Smith, Bennett, Boyle and another whose name eludes me. Smith for one might not be unaware of the dangers. It was said that his brother had been hanged for murder.

The details of the case do not matter.

What struck me as significant, apart from the vehement denial by all four that they had had any part in the victim's death was that, according to custom the prosecution in the High Court, unless in Edinburgh, and this was in Glasgow, was in the hands of Junior Counsel: in this case a conscientious, able lawyer who has since "proved" himself but who, at that time, had very very little experience. A labour Government was in power, but the situation would have been just the same under a Tory administration.

He had to do battle virtually alone. Now an author and a "silk" I shall not mention him, but I shall say that he is a delightful man for whose professional abilities I have the highest regard. Lord Stott in his book *Lord Advocate's Diary* has suggested that statistics have shown that this was not a bad practice. I can only comment that as a sportsman I should always have felt more optimistic fielding my strongest team and that I could see no logic in a murder case being prosecuted by the Solicitor-General because it happened to be in Edinburgh and by a junior of three years standing because it happened to be in Glasgow. Representing the accused, were four experienced QC's, each supported of course by junior counsel.

Battle was joined.

When each Crown witness had been examined by the young Advocate-Depute, the battery of "silks" took over. Each in his own way bombarded the witness, and any significant point which might have been missed by any of them was assuredly made by one of the others.

As witness after witness went through the witness box, the pressure on the Crown built up. There was a lesser charge against each of breach of the peace, mainly of pushing and jostling, not the sort of charge to worry any of the four accused. No one bothered about it.

Eventually, almost inevitably, the prosecution case faltered. This is not to suggest that with more experienced Crown Counsel the verdict would have been different.

We were told however that if all four were to plead guilty to breach of the peace the murder case would be dropped. A murder charge dropped if you would plea guilty to breach of the peace. Yes, thank you. You can imagine the alacrity with which this offer was accepted by all of the four in the dock.

My client, Jimmy Boyle sat quietly in the dock as the verdict of "Not Guilty" to murder was announced. So did his companions.

As they were taken below after being sentenced to three months' imprisonment each for breach of the peace their pent-up feelings were released, some were rocking with laughter. To hardened characters it was no more than a slap on the wrist.

Boyle of course, did not "retire" when he came out. Again he was accused of violence. Eventually, for the third time, to no surprise of the Glasgow public or the Glasgow police, he was arrested on a charge of murder. I was not involved.

This time he changed his solicitor and opting not for Dunlop, went to Mr Joseph Beltrami then a rising star in Glasgow amongst solicitors in the criminal field. Mr Beltrami instructed the young Mr Nicholas Fairbairn in Boyle's defence.

Boyle this time despite Nicky's brave efforts was found guilty of murder and received a life sentence.

I have never, of course, seen Boyle since defending him. I am told that he is a reformed character and has done a great deal of good work since his release from a life sentence. I am glad to hear of it.

I personally never received any form of acknowledgement or thanks for assisting him to be "free" to carry out the murder for which he was convicted although in my experience it is not unusual for those who have been acquitted of a criminal charge to show gratitude to their Counsel. Nor am I yet aware of any expression of deep remorse uttered by him since for the pain and suffering he clearly caused to so many people in his early life.

The psychiatrists and prison reformers however, seem pleased with his rehabilitation. While sceptics may abound that the leopard does not change his spots, it is not unknown for those who have been capable of great violence to show great compassion.

....

As a sad footnote, many years later when I was on the Bench I was sorry when Jimmy's son appeared before me on a drugs charge. The boy who became involved in the twilight world died young. I am sure that Jimmy must miss his son.

40.

BRIEF ENCOUNTER

It was one of those trials in which the faces of the women on the jury seem to stiffen and freeze at every sordid revelation while the men seem to have no problem in keeping awake.

You may have guessed. While the public seats were well occupied, and the press were there in strength, a number of young ladies passed through the witness-box, some hard-bitten, some beguilingly coy, each describing an occupation which tended to concentrate her presence in the bed-chamber.

Some of course mentioned a variety of other venues, until it appeared that there was no end to the number of places in which this particular activity could flourish.

Details were given of the financial charge made by each for performing an intimate personal service which apparently varied according to whether there was merely a brief encounter which was more modestly priced, or a lengthy or all-night session. It was in a generation when the market was not flooded with amateurs.

The Sheriff was ill at ease, and for some reason wished to have a break in the proceedings. A dear chap, I shall not name him.

Perhaps he might have expressed himself better.

Turning to the jury he said, "Ladies and Gentlemen I propose to rise now for a short time."

41.

PIGS DON'T FLY

Callum Wilson was a Scot, a beanpole of a man who stood 6 foot 6 inches in his kilt. His mind was hyperactive and his tongue rattled like a machine-gun. Although indulging in minor activities such as drinking copious quantities of brandy and running a gaming club, his principal business venture when I met him had to do with the breeding—some said the non-breeding—of pigs.

Callum did not have to be a farmer to know that, given the right circumstances, and of course the right partner, the pig will reproduce prolifically, and in this he foresaw the prospect of great wealth for himself.

This was to lead to a cause célèbre.

The idea behind his brainchild, Highland and Lowland Hatcheries, was that members of the public should be invited to contribute to the purchase of their own individual pigs. They would be armchair farmers. No worries about mucking out the odiferous sty, or anxieties about the dreaded erysipelas. While they sat comfortably at home the sow in which they had invested some of their hard earned savings would fatten, farrow and produce for them a huge litter of piglets. Theirs. These might be sold to their financial advantage or some—the female ones at least—might produce even more piglets.

The prospects were enough to produce not only a grunt of satisfaction but a squeal of delight. Double, treble, quadruple your capital. There might even be fourteen in a litter.

Public advertisement brought a ready response. Optimism and greed fuel the gambler. There seemed then no question of buying a pig in a poke. Housewives, businessmen, even a clergyman from Zambia and a host of others eager to increase their capital weighed in with contributions, and not just from their piggy banks.

The pigs—I suppose boars—went to work.

In order to encourage a cosy confidence in the bosom of investors they were invited generously on a Sunday afternoon, by prior arrangement of course, to visit a piggery for each to view a personally-owned pig.

It is a wise man who knows his own pig.

What, of course, was to be asserted later on, was that a number of people had the same pig pointed out to them as their own specific property not, of course, simultaneously. This is only hearsay.

Rumour began to spread, however, that all was not well down on the farm, and the authorities began to take an interest. It had nothing to do with swine fever. Mm, it was just that orthodox accounting methods appeared to differ considerably from Callum's, and the upshot was that eventually, after a number of complaints from investors who had failed to bring home the bacon, he was indicted in the High Court at Edinburgh on a charge of embezzlement—a cool £147,000. A lot in those days.

Strenuous efforts were made to persuade him to admit guilt as opposed to gilt even to a lesser amount than £147,000. He steadfastly refused. Although Callum himself was the "brains" behind the venture, his wife was charged. His brother was charged. Pressure mounted on him. There was some suggestion that if he were to plead guilty, even to part of the charge, the charge against both of them would be dropped. Callum still resisted all blandishments and refused to admit guilt. After all, if you think that you have done nothing wrong, why plead guilty?

So his solicitor, another kilted gentleman by the name of Donald McNeill McWilliam, briefed me to defend Callum.

Naively Donald had, an erroneous perhaps, but oft repeated belief that if I would "work" as he put it, there was no counsel in Scotland more likely to win a criminal case. I had handled a number of cases successfully for McWilliam. He could be a kindly man, but not to his enemies. I knew how he worked. He had never flustered himself by providing initially an excess of information but, if you asked him to follow up some line he would do his best. He was the only solicitor who brought with him to consultations in my chambers in Heriot Row his dog, a bull terrier. I remember Bimbo well.

Donald who had served in Burma during the war always assured me that he was known as the Brigade Major who never got tight.

This oft repeated message was the clear indication not only that consultation should end, but that the later consumption of whisky was filtering through and superimposing itself on the early morning intake. He sent me a lot of cases for which I was grateful. In some ways he was a likeable man whom I would have protected against his "enemies" but I doubt if I gained financially from him as much as the Distillers Company did.

Sadly Donald like many of my contemporaries has "gone to his reward".

I am always intrigued when Counsel or solicitors seek to have a case adjourned to a later date. When I received instruction to defend Callum Wilson it was a Friday. That January morning, before going into the sixth and final day of a successful divorce case, I went into the High Court to plead for breathing space. I sought an adjournment of the trial to a later date.

I told their Lordships that I had just been instructed in an involved embezzlement case which had been set down for Monday of the following week and which would last for some time, all that I wished to have was to have time for preparation

—an adjournment. I thought that in fairness to the accused my request was a valid one.

There were 667 Crown witnesses cited. There were 732 Crown productions. One of the productions in itself ran to 148 pages. I was told politely to get on with it. My motion to adjourn was refused.

I often wonder how some young practitioners would react today if so treated. Some now look aggrieved if they cannot have three weeks to answer a small Minute of Amendment.

The trial began.

Solemnly witness after witness described his or her own personal investment. Mostly I did not bother to cross examine, it was formal stuff. It was only following this particular case that in Scotland the practice of having a Minute of Admissions was introduced to the High Court whereby time and money in great quantities could be saved by both Crown and defence giving written agreement to matters which are not in contention. If only more people would avail themselves of it today what a saving in time and money.

It reminded me that just after the 1939–1945 war, when Lord Patrick, a former Dean of Faculty, who had sat with such distinction on the War Crimes Commission in Japan, chided the Advocate Depute, Robert Sherwood-Calver (later Sir Robert, QC, Sheriff Principal of Lanarkshire) who was then prosecuting and who had put a leading question to a Crown Witness in examination in chief.

"I understand, my Lord" said Calver in answer, " that the matter I put is not in dispute between myself and my learned friend for the defence".

"Mr Depute," said Lord Patrick, with the brevity and clarity which characterised his utterances, " you *may* not lead evidence in the High Court".

Until after the case I now describe this, as I say, still pertained.

The trial accordingly proceeded slowly. I was greatly indebted to Crown Counsel, the Home Depute F W F O'Brien QC, (later Sir Frederick O'Brien QC Sheriff Principal of the Lothians) in my preparation of the case each night. Following the customary fairness of the Crown he would give me a list of the particular witnesses whom he proposed to call on the following day. There was, of course, not time for my solicitor to take statements from them. All I could do after a long day in Court—we invariably sat until 5pm, having started promptly at 10am—was to spend hours with my client to ascertain from him what evidence he thought such witnesses might be able to give. Four hours sleep per night is not really quite sufficient over a period unless you are Hitler, Lord Nuffield or Lady Thatcher.

The Crown however began to have problems in its presentation, a matter which obviously did not disturb my brief sleep. Whatever the root of the trouble there were mutterings and recriminations behind the scenes.

In those days Crown Counsel changed automatically with a change in government. There were even those at the Bar who adjusted their politics in the hope that they might be included in the Crown Office team and eventually gain judicial preferment. It would be invidious to name them. High Office some achieved indeed but they are the masters of their own conscience. It took the efforts of a later Lord Advocate, Norman Wylie QC (later Lord Wylie) a man of unswerving ambition but at the same time of considerable perception to change all that.

The present case had begun in preparation while a "Tory" team was in office. The presentation in Court was handled by a "Labour" team. While, if either, was to blame if any, or, indeed, whether both were to blame, I kept spotting holes in the case. In this I received help from the two young juniors who represented Wilson's wife and brother. One was young Kenneth

Cameron, a future Lord Advocate and now the second Lord Cameron referred to by "The Times" as Cameron bouffant. The other was Neil Gow now QC and Sheriff at Ayr. My own junior was Neville Schaffer, now QC.

A blazing row developed between Crown Counsel and the presiding judge, who happened to the the first Lord Cameron. It was provoked by a question which I put to Hamish Armour CA a highly skilled accountant who was giving evidence for the Crown.

I shall spare the details.

Eventually, however, the Crown retracted from its original position. The charge was reduced dramatically from £147,000 to £63,000, still a substantial sum, which never even for a second tempted Callum Wilson to make any concession.

On and on we went to a conclusion. Callum in the end was triumphant. The jury returned with a verdict which was, to the defence, highly satisfactory.

"Mr Bell, that was great" he said. The embezzlement charge evaporated and he was fined £50 on each of two counts for not keeping his books properly. It was a time for Wilson family glee but for others to catch up with sleep. Charged with embezzling £147,000 and fined £100. Not bad.

Callum as he chattered would have given me the earth in gratitude, but I did not even get the gaming club. You see, his declared finances made it possible for him to claim the benefit of Legal Aid and from there eventually, I received some remuneration for the seventeen day trial. The fee would, I think, today, satisfy Counsel for a couple of days in the High Court but fall far short of that for one day's appearance by a busy "silk" in a public inquiry.

I was not perturbed. Two of the most able "silks" in criminal practice were then otherwise engaged. Lional Daiches QC was now a Sheriff in Glasgow, Ewan Stewart QC whose farewell party I had attended in the New Club, on the election of a Labour Government in 1964 had returned speedily from New Zealand to which he had just emigrated in 1963 to be the Solicitor-General. The other "top" criminal Counsel Nicholas Fairbairn (the late Sir Nicholas Fairbairn QC MP) and Irvine Smith later Sheriff and now since retirement from the Bar also QC, were both still juniors.

I had now on a personal note, so I was informed from a credible source, the largest "silk" criminal practice in Scotland. 1965. I was reasonably content.

You may wonder about Callum Wilson. Within days he was apparently expounding on some lucrative scheme to import goods from Holland; nothing to do with tulips from Amsterdam. Enough to make one shudder.

The privations of life in a prisoner of war camp in Germany and in Poland had not helped him.

On the German army's retreat from the east in the bitter winter of 1945 he and others had been forcibly marched, ill-clad and ill-fed, by their captors with a number of Russian prisoners who were at least as badly looked after.

As shortage of petrol forced the Germans, who were taking supplies in the other direction to the front, to use horse transport one of the horses slipped on the ice and broke a leg. It was quickly pulled out from between the shafts, and with Teutonic precision, shot.

Within no time the Russsian prisoners broke ranks and descended on it, clawing the warm flesh with their bare hands and swallowing it greedily, until little was left but bare bones, some skin and hair, and clouds of steam.

I do sympathise with men who have suffered: and Callum had. How else could he have behaved so rudely years after the war?

A group of German tourists had come ashore from a cruise liner in the Forth. Callum had learned to speak German while a prisoner and his services were called in as an interpreter.

He found himself in Edinburgh Castle showing a party round the Scottish National War Memorial. On coming outside he was approached by a small erect German with a cropped head and with "Heidelberg" scars on his cheek.

The German clicked his heels stood erect and said to Callum with every reverence and a military respect:—

"Thank you for showing us the shrine to your war dead".

Callum did not behave like a gentlemen. Standing there, 6 foot, 6 inches, in his kilt of course, he looked down hard at the German.

"Think nothing of it, you bastard" he said. "But for you, we wouldn't have one".

The German did not reply.

Poor Callum, later I saw him once from the distance in the stand at Hampden Park where I had gone with Tommy Walker, the Hearts manager, to the European Cup Winners Cup Final between Liverpool and Borussia Dortmund. The night when Bill Shankley railed to me about the "chicken" performance of one of his "strikers". Liverpool had actually lost.

Then one day much later, Callum appeared alone in a place where I was lunching.

It was a Monday when the Court of Session did not sit.

"How are you?" I said.

He was sipping a brandy, and seemed short of breath.

"Mr Bell" he confided, "I think maybe I've had a wee bit of a heart attack".

He went away.

I never saw him again, The next day, Tuesday, he dropped dead.

42.

DICING WITH DEATH

Murders in Scotland, though frequent, are not generally known for their ingenuity or imagination.

It occasioned thus no surprise when the body of a man of little means was found in a battered condition on a piece of waste ground in the east end of Glasgow. He had apparently been robbed of his few possessions.

It had been a busy evening in other ways. Celtic had played a football match in front of a huge crowd against Real Madrid, and the Central Station, its environs and the roads out to Celtic Park had in consequence been thronged.

The police began their enquiries.

Despite criticism over unsolved murders it is amazing how, with little to go on, the police are so often able to pin-point their target and to make an arrest. In the course of their numerous enquiries into this death, enquiries involving endless hours and numberless people, one man whose reputation was not untarnished was asked simply if he had been in Central Station on the night in question.

He was, at worst for him at that stage, merely a vague possible suspect or source of information, at best someone to be eliminated from suspicion. Had he said "Yes", which would have been truthful, it might have been the end of the matter for him. He chose to lie. The police in fact knew that he had been in the station, as had thousand of others that evening. Why lie? To be in a crowded fume-laden city railway station may be a more serious risk to health than inhaling someone's cigarette smoke, but it is not a crime.

If the police had reason to believe that one of the people involved in the murder—there were understood to be two— had been in the station that evening their enquiries to interview all might have taken a long time. If Charlie (I shall call him that) had come clean on his presence in the station he might as I say, have been eliminated. He did not.

I have never ceased to be astonished at how many criminals, be it in the witness box or outside of it, who would have been in a much better position if they had found it in themselves to answer even the simple and innocuous questions truthfully. They are not all pathological liars. Because Charlie told such a simple lie the police began to wonder why. Enquiries proceeded. As a result eventually he did come under suspicion for a murder which was committed some distance away from the station.

Finally, Charlie and another were charged with the murder —and significantly with robbery.

The penalty if guilty of course in those days was death if the murder were accompanied by robbery.

A jury was empanelled before Lord Wheatley and while I looked after Charlie, his co-accused was defended by Neil McVicar QC (later Sheriff McVicar in Edinburgh) who had a pleasing manner as Counsel but was not a familiar figure on the criminal circuit.

The details of the evidence are of no moment for this story.

Broadly speaking the Crown alleged that the victim's head had been used in the same manner as the ball at Celtic Park, that after a number of kicks it had shown less resilience and that, having killed their victim, the two had stolen his few trivial possessions.

For the Crown, like the defence in many such cases, the outcome, despite a mass of careful preparation and a welter of information to be translated into evidence, is never certain. Crucial information may be lost. A vital witness may go back on his statement or modify it, he may lie on a vital matter, he may plead forgetfulness, genuine or otherwise. He may simply disappear temporarily.

After a long procession of Crown witnesses the prosecuting Counsel then a promising junior, W I Stewart, Advocate Depute, (now a retired senior judge, Lord Allanbridge) approached McVicar and myself during an interval.

Such a meeting, which is not unusual of course, was totally unknown not only to both Lord Wheatley and the jury but to everyone else.

The essence of his proposal was that, if both our clients would plead guilty to non-capital murder, he would drop the charge of capital murder. The attraction to the two accused was at once obvious. Both of their necks would be safe.

McVicar and I at once repaired to the cell area to break the news to our respective clients.

I do not know exactly what transpired between McVicar and his client. Suffice it to say that he apparently accepted the suggestion with alacrity. At that stage in the proceedings he was willing to accept any suggestion which would guarantee his personal survival.

There is much to be said in favour of being alive.

When I spoke to Charlie (not his real name) he listened to me intently. The relationship of Counsel defending on a capital murder charge to his client, I have often felt, is a closer one than that of mother and son. Barring the possibility of a later reprieve, for a brief agonising period no-one stands closer to the accused than the Counsel whose astute handling on one hand, or tactical error on the other, may eventually save his life or contribute to his death.

It is a unique relationship which the modern Counsel despite a wealth of experience will never encounter,and despite an exceptional ability, will never comprehend.

As I outlined the Crown proposal to him, Charlie sat silent and motionless, listening intently.

I then gave him my professional assessment of the evidence.

There is sufficient evidence now, if the jury accept it in preference to any evidence we may lead, to convict you of murder. I do not think that the Crown can prove the robbery. If I am right, that means that at least your life is safe. Remember that lawyers are not always right. If you turn down the Crown offer and go ahead as we stand, and I am wrong, I may only lose a case but you may lose your life. Charlie sat as still as a statue and totally silent. I could not guess what thoughts were going through his mind. His exact verbatim reply came suddenly.

Frankly, I fully expected him to admit involvement and to settle for the possible loss of liberty in preference to the possible loss of life. What would you have done in his position?

Instead he looked me straight in the eye as one would look at a close and trusted friend.

His exact verbatim reply was short.

"You've done great, sir. I'll take a chance on it".

"It", as he appreciated and I knew, was his life. Flabbergasting.

I returned to find out that McVicar's client would have accepted virtually any proposal which would save him from the rope.

This presented a further problem. The offer by Crown Counsel to drop the capital charge was based on a plea of guilty to non-capital murder by BOTH. I suggested to McVicar that he should see Crown Counsel at once. Why, I suggested, should your client's life still be at risk because of the stance taken by my client? The logic was clear.

When McVicar met Crown Counsel the latter at once saw the difficulty. Very well, if McVicar's client alone pleaded guilty to non-capital murder he would accept that plea, thus ensuring his survival. Stewart was a fair man. He would accept a plea of guilty to non-capital murder from McVicar's client alone.

McVicar then repaired to convey the welcome news to his client that such a plea would be accepted on his part. The man was overjoyed.

Then a thought instinctively crossed his mind. "What about Charlie?" he asked, referring to my client.

"Oh, he's going on" said McVicar.

In this tense atmosphere what thoughts then raced through the man's mind I do not know. The possibility that he might spend years behind bars and that, by chance, Charlie might be walking about a free man? Who would know.

His answer came quickly. "If he's going on, so am I".

Negotiations were at an end. Thus the case proceeded from the precise point where it had been adjourned with the threat of death still hanging over and in contemplation by both.

Of these incidental developments of course no one else as I have said knew. The judge, the jury, the public, the press were all unaware of this little interlude which casts such an illuminating light on one tiny aspect of human behaviour.

At the end of the evidence legal submissions were made. Lord Wheatley in addressing the jury then directed them that there was insufficient evidence in law to entitle them to convict of capital murder, but sufficient to convict of non-capital murder. No rope for either.

The jury retired, considered their verdict and returned. Both men were to live, but with a restriction on their freedom for years to come.

Charlie would not know. His Counsel was also relieved if not to this same degree and went home thinking simply "Thank God, I have not defended one who went to the gallows".

43.

BELL'S AFORE YE GO

Charlotte Nicol v *Bell* is a well-known Scottish case. It is reported in 1954 *Scots Law Times.*

In case you are thinking of rushing to read it, I can save you a lot of trouble. The flavour is not to be savoured in the dry legal report but in the unlikely sequel. I was only concerned with the latter.

James Bell, not a relative of mine, need I add, was a Glasgow bookmaker. As so often with such gentlemen, he had a few sideline businesses—one, if I remember correctly, the Piccadilly Club in Sauchiehall Street, Glasgow which at one time strangely enough numbered amongst its members one of the eight Sheriffs Principal I have known to administer the area. In order to avoid embarrassment I should stress that it was not Sheriff Principal Norman McLeod QC, the seventh one who would have cut an unlikely dash in such surroundings. Nor will any prizes be awarded for guessing.

Such clubs received support mainly because in addition to food they were able to suppply alcoholic refreshment up to 11pm. The public houses were not permitted to sell after 9.30pm in Glasgow, in Paisley not after 9pm, while in liberal Edinburgh the hour was 10pm. At one minute to closing time there was a rush to supply drinks. At one minute after closing time there was a repeated shout for those who had just been supplied, to leave the premises.

Momentarily, however, we are concerned with one of James Bell's other sidelines. This was Charlotte Nicol. Let me explain.

In 1940 an Act of Parliament abolished two of the three old forms of irregular marriage in Scotland and left one standing:—Marriage by cohabitation with habit and repute.

If this seems gobble-dy-gook, let me again explain. It means roughly that if a man lived with a woman over a period of time, in this case 22 years (cohabitation) both being unmarried, provided the woman could prove that, although unmarried, she was held out to be the man's wife, and people regarded her as his wife (with habit and repute) and not just as mistress, she might raise an action of declarator in the Court of Session to have it declared that she was in fact his wife. In case any male readers should feel a nasty shock running through their systems, I repeat that the woman had to be paraded and presented as, his wife, and not just as a woman with whom he was associating. The present partners, "live in lovers", bidies-in, or whatever expression is in vogue this week, will have to take stock and consult a solicitor.

Charlotte Nicol decided, accordingly, that if James Bell would not make an "honest woman" out of her, she would do it off her own bat, or rather let the Court tie the knot. Besides, a wife has legal rights in her husband's estate and it was well known to Charlotte Nicol that James Bell did not require to live on public funds.

So, she raised an action in the Court of Session to have it declared that she was his wife. Resistance on his part was swift.

It was a long and bitter battlewhich went to appeal, but in the end she attained the marriage status without the accompaniment of Mendelsohn's Wedding March.

Enter the stage now Mrs Bell, the former Miss Nicol. It transpired that the lady had also other considerations in mind. She was not contemplating connubial bliss, a warm romantic togetherness as they sat à-deux of an evening billing and cooing by their fireside. Neither was James Bell. By this time they were unlikely to be seen together in the same room, let alone at the same fireside.

He was believed to have other fish to fry. He did not dream constantly of Charlotte. In fact it was reputed that he was not adverse to finding female company elsewhere.

Having put the marriage noose finally round his neck, Charlotte's appetite for litigation had not diminished. Encouraged by her success her next move was to raise another action against him. He was led on the lasso back to the Court of Session.

This time it was an action of separation and aliment on the ground of his adultery. After all, a lady can't have her brand new husband playing away from home.

Cool, you may think.

Such an action if successful of course would yield a double bonus. Firstly having overcome the hurdle of marrying him, she would, if granted a separation, not have the disagreeable duty of having to live with him and secondly, if successful in obtaining a legal separation she could then exact from him the sort of financial provision that would enable her to live in the standard of comfort to which she had clearly set her mind.

The best laid schemes of mice and women, however, gang aft agley.

Something went wrong. I know not what. I was not involved. Horror of horrors for Charlotte, the separation action became unstuck and collapsed. She failed to prove his adultery. It may be, of course, that he had not committed adultery.

Thus were the two of them married but now living apart and she, having elected to do so, was unable to get the Court's blessing for the income on which she had set her mind.

No man, and no money. What a ghastly situation for any lady of mature age.

Years passed, and I finally came into the picture. I had only been about four years at the Bar when the couple had their first battle in Court, and now I was a QC.

James Bell had long brooded on the fact that he faced the worst of two worlds. There was no married bliss, but she was still his wife and, as such, entitled to share of his estate should he die. He consulted his solicitors.

Solicitors are always glad to be consulted.

His wish? To divorce Charlotte on the grounds of her desertion of him. Yes, desertion. To succeed he would have to profess and to prove that for at least a period of three years after their separation he had been willing to adhere to her, i.e.. to live with her.

Cool you may think. Well, he was prepared to say so under oath.

Battle was joined. A summons was served on her and defences of course were promptly lodged. Charlotte had not forced her way in by the front door just to be thrown out of the back window. Senior and junior counsel were engaged by both parties and after pleadings had been adjusted a date was fixed for the proof.

I found Douglas Reith QC, a near neighbour in Heriot Row, on the other side and the case was put out before Lord Walker. The fight went on for four days, and believe it or not, I managed to win for James Bell his freedom—divorce. Charlotte was out—and even further out than when she had first started to litigate in 1954. No man, no money and no marriage. The very nadir of female existence unless you happen to be a lesbian communist.

Fees as I have indicated were a bit of a giggle compared with now, so I shall not tell you exactly what reward I received for saving my namesake many, many thousands of pounds. A shilling of reward.

I did not see or hear of James Bell for a long time. It seemed unlikely that our paths would cross again.

Gratitude, however, can lie dormant for a long time.

Years later, I went on a Wednesday afternoon to Clifton-hill, Coatbridge, the ground of Albion Rovers Football Club to see them play Queens Park in a Scottish Cup tie. I was not there in any partisan capacity. As a director of Heart of Midlothian I kept my eyes and my ears closely on developments in the game and any promising young blood.

Hearts, chasing the League Championship, which they eventually missed by .02 of a goal, had only one recognised experienced goalkeeper the Scottish international Jim Cruickshank, and I was anxious to appraise first, and then to get Tommy Walker our manager to run his professional eye over a young amateur whom I thought had some potential and might suit us, Bobby Clark, who was keeping goal that day for the amateur club Queens Park. (He subsequently played for many years for Aberdeen and also for Scotland). Perhaps I should have been a football scout and not a lawyer.

After the match, having chatted to local manager Bobby Flavell, an ex Hearts player, I was offered a lift back to Glasgow by Tom Fagan the Albion Rovers Chairman, an engaging character who dealt profitably in second hand motor cars and promising young footballers, and who invited me to have a meal in Glasgow with him before I caught the train to Edinburgh. I accepted. I did not know of course where he would take me.

Where else but the Piccadilly Club. Moreover, as luck would have it when I was leaving to catch my train to Edinburgh we bumped into the proprietor, my former client James Bell who happened to be on the premises.

He seemed delighted to see me after so many years, and was obviously happy at my assistance in relieving him of the burden of marriage. He disappeared with an apology but returned quickly to ask if I would accept a small present from him to tide me over on the long train journey to Edinburgh.

What else could the token of his magnanimity be?

It was a half bottle of Bell's whisky.

For lawyers who always want "specification" I should add that it was Arthur Bell's whisky and not James Bell's whisky.

I need hardly add that I reached home without this precious gift being opened. It is not however to be found amongst my souvenirs.

44.

NOTHING TO SAY

Armed bank robbery is not an especial favourite of the public, and even less so of the criminal authorities.

The successful daylight raid in the sixties on the Pollokshaws Branch of the Royal Bank of Scotland in Glasgow provoked an outcry of anger and unease.

Authority moved swiftly.

Soon three men were indicted, none of them strangely unknown to the police. Bank robbery suspects are less numerous than shoplifters, and easier to identify and locate. Their swift denial of involvement would have cut little ice with the hard-headed Glasgow police.

Walter Scott Ellis, McIntyre and Neeson were a formidable trio. So far as the police were concerned they would have used a different adjective but Ellis was top of the Premier League, a man whom it was said struck fear not only into the hearts of the public but of many hardmen in the underworld. His court experience it was said included a trial for murder after a taxi-driver was shot in the head. Not proven said the jury.

McIntyre had already served a four-year sentence for sticking a knife in a police-officer's buttock. Rumour had it jokingly that they were still searching there for the knife. Neeson was no longer an undergraduate in the university of crime.

When Ellis was charged his solicitor was quickly on to my clerk to see if I would be free to defend "Public Enemy No. 1". I was never consulted but later learned that my clerk had said that I was not available.

Within no time another solicitor was in touch to see if I would appear for McIntyre. To this request my clerk apparently said

"Yes". You may well wonder at this behind-the-scenes activity. My clerk, simply protective of me, had deemed it inadvisable that I should appear for Ellis who was described by some as the most dangerous man in Scotland. I personally would have been prepared to bear the burden.

When the case was called in court it was obvious that every police endeavour and every Crown muscle was flexed to prosecute with the utmost vigour. They wanted him put away.

The junior Advocate-Depute a fresh eager young face leading for the Crown was John McCluskey (now Lord McCluskey) who having worn the years well is now a fresh eager older face, a man of many interests who has maintained his youthful zeal in a practical fashion. He brought a cold, clinical efficiency to the proceedings to a degree which provoked one defence solicitor to suggest that he had cast himself in the mould of persecutor rather than prosecutor. Perhaps the solicitor had just seen the writing on the wall.

Presiding over the trial was "Jack" (Lord Hunter) who brought with him a large physical and mental presence, and a barely concealed distaste for the criminal classes.

"Battling Jack", not unknown to the rugby field or the war-time Royal Navy in Burma, brought with him a rugged exterior and a stamina which sustained him through endless hours of work in his study, and equally so when the top was removed from a bottle. In his earlier years after Bar dinners he had been known playfully to pour claret over a head to which he took exception, or to telephone the Isle of Lewis to enquire after the health of one Boris Miller the Sheriff at Stornoway.

His ability as a lawyer I can vouch for, having often appeared as his junior, was never in doubt. His humour was never far away even when noisily interrupted by the electors of Shettleston who spurned his attempts to reach Parliament.

When conducting the inquiry into the famous "Thurso Boy" case in Inverness he was heard to remark dryly while walking down the steps with the full glare of the television cameras upon him "This won't do. My friends in London think that I'm a Mr Smith from Birmingham"

It was clear from the outset that the "hard" trio in the dock had not arrived at a picnic, and that neither Lord Hunter nor McClusky was there to offer sandwiches.

Brick by brick, no matter what burrowing instrument we produced in defence the Crown edifice stood firm and grew bigger and stronger. When their case closed it looked unassailable.

Any hope of escape for McIntyre clearly rested on his going into the witness-box, playing down or denying his own involvement. A tall order and, with every truth, lie or histrionics he could muster, being believed by the jury. This I told him in the plainest terms. I did not of course tell him to lie, but was aware that his instincts might lead him in that direction.

Most people on a serious criminal charge are prepared to take their counsel's advice and to say or do anything which may exculpate them irrespective of the truth or the damage it may do to others—even their fellow-accused.

My clear advice to McIntyre however fell on deaf ears. Had he given up hope, had he not minded being convicted? Certainly not.

The reason why McIntyre would not go into the witness-box was quite simple. He was afraid that, if he gave evidence, he might unwittingly in cross-examination say something that might inculpate Ellis. Worse, he was afraid that, even if he did not say anything which would inculpate Ellis, that Ellis might interpret any evidence he gave as a contributing factor to a conviction of Ellis.

It is unusual for a criminal to appear more concerned with the escape of a fellow-accused than his own. In cases without number the accused will pour out a torrent of words and "rat" on his accomplices without hesitation if this will help to save his own trembling skin.

For McIntyre the decision to say nothing in evidence was indeed determined by self-interest as one might expect, but of a very different kind. Simply this.

It was his belief that if he were held by Ellis to be in any way responsible for the conviction of Ellis, Ellis would kill him. He would gladly risk a long prison sentence as an alternative to that. The inevitable thus happened. All three were convicted.

It was time for Lord Hunter to consider the evidence in the light of the jury's verdict and to pass sentence.

One aspect of it had not escaped attention. It was said that, even after the robbery had been effected, and the accused were about to make their get away without hindrance, Ellis discharged a firearm through glass in the direction of a male bank employee. Without intervention of the glass it was said that the man might have been killed.

Lord Hunter had something to say. He proceeded to pass by far the longest sentences it had been my experience as a counsel to hear.

Ellis was sentenced to twenty-one years imprisonment. McIntyre, my client, was sentenced to eighteen years imprisonment, Neeson to a substantial but lesser period of imprisonment.

I do not know if it is true but, according to a police escort, as he was taken down Ellis is alleged to have said in his astonishment and anger:— "Hm, you get a lifer for murder, twenty-one years for that. Next time I'll kill the bastard". It may be then that my client McIntyre's worst fears were not unfounded.

In this case I seemed to have had not one but both hands tied behind my back while seeking to defend him. Perhaps I should not have sought to censure myself as strangely my conscience would make me do if unsuccessful. McIntyre, a resilient fellow, was not only able to serve his eighteen sentence in addition to his previous four, but many years later, after I had left the Bar, I am told had the resource to collect a further sentence of twelve years imprisonment without the shadow of Ellis hanging over him or the burden of my advice.

I do not know whether he had anything to say on that occasion.

Having endured the most resounding disaster—in terms of result—in my professional career I might have been forgiven had I echoed the words of the man in the public gallery who reacted to Lord Keith's sentence of ten years' imprisonment when three had been expected "Oh, for f—k's sake".

Instead, like McIntyre, I had nothing to say.

45.

JUDICIAL SEPARATION

Lord Mackintosh, a First War Royal Scot, M.C., former Barbarian Rugby footballer and a determined golfing partner when we played together, was listening with little relish while a pawky little man of 5 feet 4 inches from the east end of Glasgow gave evidence in an adultery case. A recumbent posture, the subject matter before him, and the dramatis personae, must have seemed a poor alternative to His Lordship to striding round the golf course in his home town of Nairn or at Muirfield. Though latterly failing eyesight was a problem, his mind was clear.

He might even have preferred, as was his wont, to march purposefully up the Mound on a bitter-cold winter day without an overcoat, or even a mackintosh, while other travellers heavily muffled huddled in the warmth of bus, tram, or car.

On one such day, thrusting his umbrella in front of him, he passed and re-passed the crawling traffic, and gave great amusement to tramcar passengers who observed that he not only lacked an overcoat, but that his high-peaked stiff white collar was inadvertently unadorned by the customary accompaniment of a neck-tie. A kind of judicial separation.

Now the little man in front of him, who would have been more at home without a tie, was testifying in firm, clear terms for the pursuer who sought not only judicial separation but divorce.

The witness described how he was on one side of a wooden partition while hidden from view on the other side were a couple *in flagrante delicto* as they would say over in the Gorbals.

His Lordship, who had been eyeing the little man in silence, suddenly bared his fangs like a Japanese soldier and interjected:—

"But if you were on the other side of this wooden partition, how do you know that they were having sexual intercourse?"

The little man, his credibility suddenly in question, drew himself up to his full 5 foot 4 inches.

"How dae I ken they were having intercourse?" he expostulated indignantly.

"Man, ye could have heard them peching (panting) at Parkhead Cross".

His Lordship made no further interjection and the pursuer was granted decree of divorce.

Note: Proof of adultery may not depend on the witness having X-ray eyes or even on it having actually occurred. In another case where a couple were discovered in bed together the defence that they were about to have intercourse, but were prevented from doing so by the untimely interruption of two private detectives who burst into the bedroom, was repelled. This was quoted as getting the worst of both worlds.

46.

THE MUIRHOUSE TENT MURDER

"There's an awfy smell aboot here".

Two workmen were cleaning up in a camp site at Muirhouse, Edinburgh when one conveyed the message received from his nostrils to his friend. There seemed to be a lot of insects about as well. The camp was used by visitors and holiday makers who came and went regularly without anyone knowing much about them. There was no register in such a place to record when Mr and Mrs Smith had booked in or out.

On poking their noses inside a small tent the workmen were horrified at what they saw. There lay, in a degree of putrefaction, the body of a young girl. Lying amongst her few possessions a grim ironic relic, was William Golding's well-known book "Lord of the Flies".

The police wasted no time in being involved.

In a place like this, with a population that changed every day, and people going about their own affairs without regard to whatever else might happen, the task of unravelling what had clearly been a murder—the dead girl had been strangled— was a daunting one.

From papers still there, they were able to establish that she was an American citizen, the daughter of a woman there of little political significance but of known left-wing sympathies.

Later it was ascertained that she had apparently arrived on her own in Scotland from Iceland with the customary sleeping-bag and other paraphernalia with which youth are now wont to travel fearlessly on their own about the world. It later transpired also that on arrival she had camped out in Queen Street Gardens, opposite Abercromby Place, and spent a night there alone.

Next day she had moved slightly south to Princes Street where she met a young man and lay for part of the day in the gardens with him smoking cannabis. They had not of course been formally introduced.

Police enquiries as to anyone who might have known or seen them continued to draw a blank. As so often, however, police leads do not come from shrewd and painstaking detective work or from informers, but by sheer chance. This was such a case.

Chief Superintendent Ronald Clancy, the head of CID in Edinburgh who had forsaken as the son of a regular soldier picking up cushions at the Oval in his youth to see desert service with the Coldstream Guards, was surprised but delighted to receive an unexpected call from the police in Southern Ireland. It was time for him to celebrate with a large gin.

It appeared that in a remote part of the Republic they had detained a young man who might possibly be of interest in Edinburgh. He had gained employment there a short time before as a commis chef. Foolishly, he had allowed himself to be arrested and charged with theft.

On going through his possessions they found some papers and articles which appeared to link him at some time with the name of the girl who had been found dead at Muirhouse. Eventually after a number of other enquiries he was brought to Scotland and soon charged with murder.

It became abundantly clear that he had been with the girl in Princes Street Gardens and, that as he himself later admitted, he had gone with her to a tent in the camp at Muirhouse. He had even slept in the same tent he said.

Smoking cannabis he admitted. Murder he strenuously denied.

When I was briefed to defend him it seemed that in the light of all he had admitted there was little room for manoeuvre. There he was admittedly alone in a tent with a girl. The girl is strangled and he disappears.

What was apparent about their relationship was the significant part played by smoking "pot". Today the presence of people in Court to answer charges of using, or supplying for use, a variety of drugs is commonplace. Then it was unusual. Even in the case of cannabis which many—not myself—argue should be legalised. In a society which is changing out of recognition to older people one imagines that it will be legalised. Now, when it may be obtained cheaply or freely by children outside school gates with less fuss than an octogenarian will receive when he lights a cigarette, one wonders at society's priorities.

I began to explore the possibility of the girl's death, even assuming it to be at his hand, to be accidental or unintentional. It was certainly not suicide.

It may seem odd now, but at that time in order to get expert advice on such a drug yes—only cannabis—I had to ferret very far afield. In the end on my advice the head of the Chelsea Research and Addiction Centre in London was called in.

I did not of course wish to "dope" the jury but only to throw a little "grass" (a name they have for the drug) if not in their eyes, then in their ears. In the drug scene of the nineties it may sound naive, but of course it is like blaming a first-war general for the slaughter involved in taking fifty yards of ground when no general in any country at that time thought of acting otherwise.

The theory propounded was this. If, for example, you swallow a quantity of drink and commit a crime you cannot turn round and say "Please, it wasn't my fault. I had been drinking and didn't have control of myself". The effects of alcohol are predictable and widely known and, if a person puts himself in such a condition by consuming it that he is not aware of what he is doing, he cannot readily escape the consequences.

What was suggested here in defence was that cannabis was smoked by people in order to create a mild euphoria. It was not known by the general public or those who used it to produce any of the results which may follow from addiction, for example, to heroin, cocaine or LSD. But, said our expert from London, he had found, in the course of his researching and dealing even with cannabis users, some startling consequences from an excessive use of it. He had known, for example, of one patient who went to an open window, stepped over it, put his arms out in the belief that he could fly and, in the event, had simply fallen like a stone twenty feet to the ground below.

What was suggested here was that there was no direct evidence to support the Crown case that the accused had murdered. Even if the jury were to come to the view that no one else could have been responsible for her death, which was not inevitable on the evidence led, the accused had not been proved to have formed a criminal intent and would have no means of knowing he had done so.

If hallucinated without the knowledge that he might be, he would have had no reason to know what had happened and he would have been unable to form any intention—which he strongly resisted having—of causing her death.

If he had no intention to kill her, and no knowledge even of how she came to die, how could he be guilty of wilfully killing her? It had been wrong of him to depart and leave her of course, but that did not make him a murderer. He had simply panicked on seeing her dead and made off.

The jury retired.

It is very difficult when the defence has one hand tied behind its back at the beginning.

The jury returned a verdict of Guilty and he received a life sentence. I personally had no complaint.

It was whispered afterwards that the police in Sussex had been taking some interest in him in view of the death of a girl in Brighton which manifested some similarities to the present case.

47.

AXED

Bernard was a woodcutter, a big, strong fellow from Brechin in the north-east. He was a bachelor and lived in a council house with his father and his father's housekeeper, a woman whose manner he disliked and whose presence he suffered with growing resentment.

It was Bernard's habit of a Saturday evening, one by no means unusual in Brechin as well as other parts of the country, to loose the inhibitions and forget the frustrations of the week, by generous patronage of some local hostelries. In this he was joined by a crony who lived nearby.

So, following their well-established custom he and his friend on a particular Saturday night did their accustomed rounds. There was nothing special or spectacular about this particular Saturday evening and having consumed, each, fourteen pints of proper live beer, not pasteurised gassy lager in those days, the two climbed the hill with less speed and less certainty of movement to their respective homes.

Bernard's father was still out, but Margaret, the housekeeper, was not. Not for the first time an altercation took place. Bernard's temper rose and in a white heat of rage he set his seal of disapproval on the whole relationship with her.

Leaving his house again he lurched down the road and knocked on the door of his friend's house. When his friend opened it he announced:—

"I've just hacked auld Maggie's heid aff".

For a moment his friend caught his eye until, looking downwards, be saw in Bernard's hand his woodcutter's axe, blood stained, while clinging to it were wispy strands of grey hair.

Without a moment's hesitation his friend brushed past him and, fearing the worst, made what speed he could to Bernard's house.

There indeed lay, in a pool of blood, auld Maggie.

The report of her condition was only wrong in one minor detail: her head was still to a slight degree attached to her body, but in a manner which clearly indicated that her end had been sudden.

Bernard was arrested and charged with murder.

When I was instructed by local solicitors through Freddie Main WS, a well known and astute Edinburgh criminal practitioner and solicitous protector of many law-breakers, to defend him, I was presented with a number of statements which bore to support Bernard's initial intimation.

In addition, I was presented with two medical reports of Bernard's mental condition, obtained from the Crown, both of which indicated that he was insane and unfit to plead. If they were to be accepted in Court then there was only one disposal for Bernard—incarceration in a State mental hospital unrestricted in point of time.

The essence of advocacy of course is to do the best for one's client, to make the worse appear the better cause and, like a general in the field, if realising that the battle cannot be won, to get out at the lowest possible cost.

While to many it might have seemed a formality, I instructed Main that two further reports should be obtained from medical experts as to his mental condition.

I further specified that these should be obtained from different parts of the country, and that care should be taken to ensure that neither expert was aware of the other's involvement, nor of the opinions already expressed by the experts instructed by the Crown. Thus I hoped optimistically to acquire two new and totally independent opinions.

Freddie, as usual wasted no time, as was his wont in driving FM7.

Having read the Crown reports, I must confess that I regarded the likely substance of the reports which I had ordered as a formality, and that they would simply confirm the views already expressed.

Those who practice law should be immune from surprise.

In the fullness of time two fresh reports reached me; each, formed independently of the other, and without a sight of the Crown reports, announced:—

"He is sane and fit to plead".

It was time to go to Court.

The Advocate-Depute was an able and rising Counsel who might well have been Lord Advocate had the Labour Party returned to power an election sooner. Donald Macaulay was a sturdy sensitive man from Lewis who contributed a fine knowledge of the law with an appreciation of association football and a good malt whisky.

The Crown led evidence of insanity in bar of trial. They wanted him to be found "Not Guilty" on the basis that he was insane and unfit to plead. I wanted him to be found guilty on the basis that, even if responsible for the killing, he was sane but should be found guilty, not of murder but of culpable homicide, on the basis that he was suffering from diminished responsibility. This, if proved, would generally attract a lighter sentence and a fixed sentence.

A strange murder case. The Crown seeking a verdict of Not Guilty and the defence seeking a verdict of Guilty.

We proceeded.

I was successful, if that is the right word, in obtaining a Guilty verdict.

In the end of the day, however, here indeed was a Pyrrhic victory.

In sentencing him Lord Avonside, having regard to the provisions contained in the Mental Health Acts, felt it appropriate to order his detention in a State mental hospital, His Lordship, as he was wont to do, coughed deeply and despatched my client with a brief growl. Not quite as deep a growl as he emitted when an Irish caddy moved and clanked some clubs as he was addressing a golf ball at Royal Portrush, or at a dinner in the New Club after a golf match in which a single Irish opponent seemed reluctant to rise to toast the Queen.

Thus Bernard was not given a definite term of imprisonment which would have meant his release at the end of a fixed period, but finished up exactly as he would have done if he had been held to be Not Guilty.

I could not complain. I had of course obtained the verdict which I sought.

48.

TO BE OR NOT TO BE

It was a raw, wet day in the bleak outback of Lanarkshire.

In the brickworks at Shotts men, bent against the elements, hurried and scurried like drenched ants to finish their day's labours and seek a more comfortable alternative. In the yard, however, one man stood quietly alone, heedless of the unremitting rain and of all the haste around him. He was dressed in a bulky raincoat, or what appeared to be a bulky raincoat. He was waiting for someone.

Although he had then no valid reason to be on the premises, his surroundings were familiar. Until that morning Joe McGonigle, a red-haired Irishman, had had every reason to be there. In fact, he might have been in trouble had he not been there, because Joe was employed in the brickworks. That is until that morning. It was now five o'clock in the evening but earlier on, about eleven o'clock, Joe had had a Hibernian of an altercation with the management. As a result he saw the works manager and was told to "collect his books" and to go. Joe was sacked on the spot.

Now, many hours later, he had come back to see someone. The person for whom he waited so patiently in the downpour was the works manager. Joe had not come back to apologise or to seek re-instatement in his job, though doubtless he regretted the loss of it.

As he waited silently near the gate, at last a car approached it from the inside. The one for which he had waited so long. It was driven by the works manager.

When he recognised Joe the driver rolled down the car window and demanded in a voice of mingled surprise and displeasure. "What are you doing here?" Joe was to provide an instant answer, but not one which would provide any opportunity for argument.

Pulling back his raincoat he at once revealed the reason for the bulkiness of his figure. From it emerged swiftly the barrel of a loaded shotgun. Without more ado he fired firmly at short range through the open window killing his inquisitor instantly.

Joe, not surprisingly, was arrested and charged with murder.

The importance of the case lies not in these stark simple facts, for violent murders are not uncommon.

The significance of the case was that it was unique in Scottish legal history.

The penalty for murder when Joe perpetrated this killing was still death. Parliament however had been busy before this and, after fierce debate, legislation had at last been introduced to abolish the death penalty for murder. The Murder (Abolition of Death Penalty) Act 1965 had not yet, however, come into force and, as matters stood, if found guilty of murder Joe was liable then to be hanged by the neck until he was dead.

The Crown Authorities however, in their wisdom delayed the date of Joe's trial until the new Act had become operative and the penalty for murder had, by the time he was brought to Court, been changed to what is erroneously termed life-imprisonment. It would clearly not have been public policy to hang anyone on the eve of the abolition of the death penalty.

It is curious to reflect now that, prior to this case, in Scotland as distinct from England, the Crown would never accept a plea of guilty in a murder charge. In England where the accused was allowed to plead guilty the solemnities had included little more, sometimes, than the judge donning a black cap and passing sentence of death. In Scotland, by contrast, the Crown insisted on proceeding to trial with a plea of Not Guilty and insisted on leading evidence to establish guilt. They were anxious to show in open Court that justice had been done; perhaps to dispel the thought that the alleged perpetrator might be considered not mentally responsible for his actions, or that the man in the dock was not an undetected Sydney Carton prepared to pay the price of another's freedom with his own life.

Having been instructed to appear in the High Court on Joe's behalf I went off to Barlinnie Prison to have a consultation with him. Really a formality. We sat down at opposite sides of a bare table while I considered what I would say to him. Or more interestingly, he to me.

It was not like the usual meetings Counsel had in Barlinnie with men on a murder charge. I had not been armed with a sheaf of statements on which to question the accused and to hear a man sometimes ready to say anything if he thought it might help his cause. I did not start with my usual pre-amble in a murder case which would have been to warn the accused that I was going to ask him a number of questions—that he was not to waste my time, or his, by giving answers which he thought might help, but to tell me the plain truth. "Remember" I would say, "that if your answers to me are lies, your defence will be based on lies and it will fall apart". "Now", I would say "Tell me...." Thereafter I would fire question after question at an accused in such a way that he had little time for concoction.

It was not like that in Joe's case. He was aware, I was aware, my instructing solicitor who was present was also aware that Joe had committed this murder. Joe himself said so and there was ample other evidence. After a few innocuous questions to gain his confidence I slipped the question in quickly and quietly.

"Why did you do this?"

He looked at me for a second, then his head turned sharply at right angles for a moment towards the little barred window which was the only source of daylight. The sun had turned its back on both of us and on the warder who stood beyond. He straightened again, looked into my face and said in a firm Irish brogue "I was angry".

Quick to my mind was the obvious thought that his was a particular anger. He had not killed while defending himself, he had not killed suddenly in a fit of temper. He had gone home. He had taken out a shotgun and loaded it. Hours later he had come back and stood passively in the rain with murder in his heart against the man who had dismissed him. A cold, calculated, patient but intense anger.

There was only one penalty for the judge to impose. Life imprisonment to which he was duly sentenced. I do not know how many years Joe served and what became of him. Of course that is not his real name.

I do know that my client was the first person ever to my knowledge in the High Court in Scotland to tender an unqualified confession to a brutal premeditated killing and, without recourse to the rejection of Crown evidence, or the benefit of any recommendation for clemency, escape with his life. When he did so he was totally unaware that the law was about to change, or of the accruing benefit to himself.

Had Joe McGonigle committed this murder even a short time before, I doubt whether he would have been alive much longer after this interview.

The debate on the death penalty will continue to rear its head from time to time.

In Europe not only the noose but the guillotine and the garrotte have been rendered idle and the death penalty obsolete. In the United States in some parts capital punishment has existed, been abolished, and re-introduced. The wheel has turned full circle, involving in the United States the barbaric practice of keeping a man on "death row" for upwards of a decade before executing him. In some African states and in the Arab world the wheel has never moved, for capital punishment has never been considered other than appropriate for murder in certain cases.

This is not the place to develop the moral argument for or against the right to take human life which is disputed by many of high moral tone in opposite camps, nor is it time to forget the most compelling of all arguments against capital punishment based simply on the fallibility of the judicial process.

The recent appeal in England in the case of Derek Bentley has revived the argument. This is not the place to develop speculation but I have the greatest doubt that, even if found guilty of murder, Derek Bentley would have been hanged if tried in Scotland.

Since the layman always has two stock questions on this subject to put to Counsel I shall answer both as experience has dictated to me.

Question 1:   How can you defend a man on a murder charge when you know he is guilty?

Answer: Mr McGonigle is the only person I have appeared for in a murder case whom I knew, or should I say believed before hand, to be guilty.

Question 2:   Are you in favour of capital punishment?

Answer: I am not "in favour of" taking human life. The question is wrongly posed. If the question were put thus, "Are you in favour of the death penalty being retained in Scotland for certain classes of murder my answer would have to be "Yes". This answer is based (a) on the safeguards built into the Scottish legal system and (b) my observation of human behaviour round the world over a long period.

The verdict of a Scottish jury does not require to be based, as in England, on unanimity or near unanimity. No 12–0 or even as now at least 10–2. The verdict of the fifteen who comprise a Scottish jury may be unanimous. It may be by majority as close as 8–7.

If a man were convicted of a capital murder by a majority verdict such a 8–7 it is inconceivable that he would be executed. If the Secretary of State for Scotland were considering the question of reprieve, and having to make recommendations, he would have before him, amongst other information, the presiding judge's report. If it were to contain, as it undoubtedly would, information about the conviction being by such a majority, which is not generally made public, it seems certain that the man would be reprieved, thus giving effect to the possibility of error as evinced by the views of a number of doubting jurors. This is a real cushion although, it must be conceded, not a complete safeguard against the error of human fallibility.

So far as the second point is concerned, those against retention of capital punishment in any shape or form will argue that statistics—the uncomprehending use of which frequently makes me shudder—statistics in the hands of people who look simply at the figures are like a loaded weapon in the hands of children - will demonstrate that capital punishment does not act as a deterrent. In a large number of cases I would believe that to be true. In others, however, if it were looming in the background I cannot but think that some might pause before embarking on any action which might involve the taking of a human life.

It is not only during a war that people find the instinct of self-preservation asserting itself. Think, for example, of the number of cowardly attacks with knives, sticks, boot or bottle by a gang of youths on another. Had any of such assailants the certain knowledge that if the victim died he might hang, might not he back off before the last fatal blows went in? Like one murder case I was in, the Abbeyhill Ballroom case in Edinburgh, where, not content with rendering the victim senseless by punching and kicking, an attacker finally jumped on the man's face crushing it inwards and breaking his nose so that eventually he drowned in his own blood.

Even to save one life in this way would be a bonus, and it might save a number if the potential murderer knew of the possible consequences to himself, simply by having capital punishment on the statute book.

The debate continues. As we become more and more "civilised" and larger sections of the populace less amenable to discipline the murder rate will not, I imagine, fall appreciably. The constant, dreary depiction of violence on television will do nothing to halt it. On the contrary. Anyone who has sat on a criminal bench over the years must have spotted the copycat attacks that are translated to the real world. While some politicians, criminologists and others do not accept this, their arguments have little relevance to those who have watched and listened over a long number of years—at first hand.

Paradoxically, while the majority of the public in fact by an overwhelming majority will continue to favour the re-introduction of capital punishment, there seems to be not the remotest likelihood that Parliament will re-introduce the death penalty.

Joe McGonigle was simply the first of many in Scotland to benefit from the age of "enlightenment".

In this he had a clear advantage over the works manager of the brickworks in Shotts.

49.

FIRE! FIRE!

After a bit of murder, rape, sodomy, incest, fraud or embezzlement it is pleasant to have a change. To be healthy one should vary one's diet. So my instruction to appear for the defence in the High Court in Glasgow on a charge of wilful fireraising (in England known as arson) brought—dare I say it—light relief.

The Crown theory of my client Wilkins was that he was a Walter Mitty type. A man born to a hum-drum existence who yearned for the headlines. Not such as that one reported in the South Wales Echo "Bus on fire—Passengers Alight", but the sort of headline which would reveal this ordinary hum-drum little man as a hero.

The thrust of the Crown case was this. Wilkins who was engaged as a night watchman, a comparatively young man, had decided to seek publicity by starting a fire in the premises which he was meant to guard. No one except himself would know that he had started the fire but, by his own courage and prompt action, he would extinguish it and thus be applauded for his heroism.

However, the fire having started, events did not develop that way. That a fire had started was certain—the whole place was soon ablaze. Whatever attempt Wilkins may have made to put it out he failed dismally. The fire took hold and caused considerable damage.

When police enquiries were complete, Wilkins was charged with having started it deliberately. This of course he denied.

It was my first encounter with David McNee, then a Chief Inspector in Dunbartonshire (who later, after Glasgow, became Sir David McNee, Chief of the Metropolitan Police in London).

McNee gave his evidence with care and clarity and soon the crown case began to look formidable.

It was time if ever to seek, before it was too late, the sympathy of the jury. This can be a delicate business. Sarcasm or bullying which may seem the most adjacent weapons on occasion to bend an unimaginative or inflexible witness are dangerous tools, and to be avoided if possible. Juries are ordinary men and women and often they do not like to see others being subjected to the kind of treatment which they know in their hearts they would hate in private life to have inflicted on themselves. They can grow to have a fellow feeling for the witness. This I wanted to avoid.

The witnesses however, whom I wanted to "destroy" were two detective officers who spoke at length, corroborating each other in rubber-stamp fashion about an alleged confession made to them by the accused.

It was vital that the jury should not believe their evidence. In examination-in-chief it was neat, glib and at first sight unshakeable. If you study a witness for long enough, however, and each of them gave me time, it is interesting to find how a line of cross-examination suggests itself.

Here were two similar, unctuous, inflexible men who would conceive it their duty to concede absolutely nothing. The obvious thing was to start by latching onto the trivia of their evidence. The sort of matters which, if conceded, or watered down, would do virtually nothing to diminish the strength of the Crown case. Police officers under cross-examination are generally defensive from the start. Thus, when they remained totally immovable on these, and failed to concede the obvious, the laymen on the jury could see at once they were following a path which would have raised the eyebrow of the simplest person.

In addition, by showing not the slightest concession or

resilience on such matters, they left themselves nothing in reserve. They reminded one of watching that delightful man and beautiful swinger of a golf club John Panton now Honorary Professional to the Royal and Ancient in the first round of the Open Golf Championships at St. Andrews. As he hung firmly and for ages over a smallish putt I thought—but even if you were doing really well, what would you have in reserve when the crunch came in the fourth round.

So with each of the detectives I was able to force up the scale of pressure as they moved into the "final round". When it became apparent to me that the jury must have seen through them, and must be on my side, I was able to use stronger weapons. Yes, even sarcasm and bullying. The jury by this time wanted to see them brought down a peg or two.

Brevity I have said so often is a good weapon in cross-examination. Not always. After grilling each for some forty-five minutes, not too long, I sat down.

The jury were with me.

Wilkins considerably against the initial odds was found not guilty of the charge.

50.

CASHING IN

Solicitors representing an accused who was about to go on trial for his life would naturally seek out an experienced criminal Counsel and, if his diary enabled him to do so, he would generally respond.

Thus I came to accept instructions for a capital murder in the High Court in Glasgow. I should perhaps explain that apart from receiving no fees I was out of pocket not only for my expenses, but had also turned down a paid engagement for the same period. The accused was an eighteen year-old youth with no money.

The murder itself was in Glasgow, and a brutal one at that.

An old woman in Maryhill had been attacked while alone in her kitchen. It was alleged that two youths were responsible and that one of them, in the course of the robbery they were said to be effecting, had picked up a carving knife and had practically cut her head off.

I was instructed on behalf of the elder of the two who was unfortunately old enough to hang if convicted. Capital murder. My junior was Stuart Kermack (later Sheriff Kermack in Forfar but now retired). The other who was only seventeen and consequently not liable to capital punishment, was represented by Irvine Smith then a highly capable and experienced young junior Advocate (now Sheriff Irvine Smith QC) who, I recall, spent his last four days in practice in October 1963 as my junior in a divorce case in the court of Session before proceeding to a seat on the Glasgow Bench.

We proceeded to trial.

The photographs of the poor woman were so horrifying that the Crown spared the jury a sight of them. The defence certainly did not allude to them. It appeared that the only financial gain from this callous killing was 1/7 (some 8p).

Eventually having heard all the evidence, the various speeches, and the charge by the presiding judge, the jury retired to consider their verdict.

For the other accused, although his life was not in peril, you can imagine the fear with which he awaited the verdict. The actual duration of a "life" sentence in terms of service might be eight or nine years at that time but it was still a sizeable slice of a young life. What my own client felt at that moment I do not know. I myself sat in a kind of numb trepidation.

As any Counsel would, I had a fierce desire never to have a man whom I defended sentence to death. It was, however no longer in my hands. A jury had to decide.

The jury returned. The younger of the two, Irvine Smith's client, was found "guilty". When the Clerk asked for the verdict in my client's case I felt more tense than ever. There was a seemingly eternal pause before the foreman of the jury announced in clear terms "Not Guilty".

I sighed and inwardly relaxed while the verdict sank in. Not so my client. In a trice, however, he was not only out of the dock but out of sight. He did not even stop to say to me either "Good-bye" or "Thank you". He was gone. I had so much wanted, indeed expected, to have a word with him and asked my junior, Kermack to see if he could be found. Kermack departed and soon returned.

No chance.

My lines in the play had been spoken, and the next scene was already being enacted elsewhere. With his family, none of whom I had met, he was already locked in hard negotiations, firstly with the Daily X and secondly with the Daily Y, as to who would pay most for his "story".

The Daily X won, and soon its pages were emblazoned with

the graphic story of Tommy Bloggs (the name is fictitious) "the boy who killed for 1/7".

It seemed astonishing that a national newspaper should make such a crass blunder. Of course Tommy Bloggs had not killed for 1/7. He had just been found not guilty of murder.

So far the fates had been kind to Tommy Bloggs. He had firstly, at no financial cost to himself or the state, escaped the possibility of the noose by being acquitted of capital murder and, secondly, he had managed to line his pocket in consequence by the publication of his "story". When Hector McKechnie QC next day drew my attention in Parliament House to the "story" I wondered what might happen next.

Days passed.

Then his agent wrote instructing me, without suggestion of a fee of course, to advise on a claim of damages against the very newspaper which had paid him, on the ground of defamation. It seemed unbelievable.

I was glad to be of help of course. That is Counsel's duty.

Having regard to his history and the whole background however, I could not bring myself to believe that his injured feelings were worth a great deal, or that they would have found an echo of sympathy in a Scottish jury. Nor am I a supporter of "telephone number" damages awards.

This was 1962. I simply told them to ask the Daily X for £250. This they paid like lambs. For a different client I might have pushed a lot harder and the newspaper might have been ready to pay more, but I doubt if a Scottish jury in the circumstances would have been much more forthcoming.

It then occurred to somebody, that in the light of the part I had played in all these proceedings that perhaps Mr Bell QC should get something for his trouble. A shilling of reward?

In an impetuous display of generosity I was sent a cheque for £10.

51.

WHAT'S IN A NAME

Sheriff James Irvine Smith, Queen's Counsel, of whom you have already heard, when on the Bench was frequently black of countenance with a scowl to match his thick black hair and large black moustache. Although a small man his voice boomed like a foghorn sounding on the Firth of Clyde and might well, had he been so minded, have carried across it to the Isle of Bute where he had his second home. His scowl was reserved only for displeasure. Socially he was benign and relaxed. He was happy dwelling on the history of Scots law, happy making an after-dinner speech, generally adapted from his filing system to provide a brand of humour appropriate to wide-ranging audiences, but if the speech were on Robert Burns he could be quite brilliant. He was equally at home with a fishing-rod or a shotgun in his hand.

As a young junior at the bar he was frequently seen to advantage in criminal cases where his reverberating rhetoric was guaranteed to keep every juror awake. Jurors like a number of others in court do not always stay awake. Only once did he have difficulty in communicating his views to the Bench. Having appeared in front of the late Sheriff-Principal Lillie QC., in Dunfermline, who was so deaf that, had he worn an ear trumpet and had a cannon discharged beside it, he would not even have blinked, Lillie remarked later that he would be quite a good counsel if he would only speak up.

It was on the Bench, however, that Irvine Smith turned up the full volume and released his wrath in mounting decibel strength on petrified criminals for whom he had acquired a deep and abiding distaste. Many a quaking evil-doer who appeared before him was glad to leave the dock and escape to the comparative comfort and safety of the cell to which he was inexorably destined.

One unfortunate wretch, however, whom he had just sentenced to a modest three months' imprisonment for breach of the peace, it was alleged, was bold or foolish enough to snap back at him defiantly: "Hm, I can do that standing on my head".

"Well," Irvine is alleged to have said in a trice, "You can have another three months for contempt of court, and that will give you time to find your feet".

No wonder that amongst many below waiting to be brought up for sentence there were anxious enquiries as to whether he was on the Bench.

So it happened one day that when two old lags were waiting below to be dealt with, rumour had it that Sheriff Smith was on the Bench. Rumour is not always reliable and on this day was misleading. Indeed, it was a Sheriff Smith, but the incumbent that day was a lady, Sheriff Laura Smith, now since her marriage, Sheriff Duncan in Glasgow, who was not related to the scourge of the underworld. What neither of the two "villains" knew was that she, a keen sailor in her leisure moments, was disposed, if the mood took her, to dish out sentences stiffer than an ocean breeze.

When the first of the two was brought up, his spirits were raised momentarily by the absence of Sheriff Irvine Smith. He was, however, unaware of the danger embodied in the sturdy presence of Sheriff Laura Smith. His joy was short-lived as he was handed out a real Smith-like sentence.

As he made his way down in a shattered condition he passed his fellow "villain" who was on the way up. Anxiously the latter asked "Is it Irvine Smith?"

"No" growled the former acidly. "He sent his F—ing wife".

52.

BUTTERFLY'S WING

"They're aye cryin' oot for justice, and when they get it, they dinna want it". This penetrating observation was spat out by an old crone in Edinburgh's High Street to her companion in gossip as she glanced down with approval at a newspaper billboard which screamed out "Court sentences nine year old girl to detention". It was September 1973 and one of the most sensational cases in years had just exploded. A nine year old girl charged with attempted murder.

In Scotland a person may be held criminally liable at the age of eight, in England at ten, and in a number of European countries not until the teens.

While Scots, even in their most immodest moments, would not argue that the reason is that they develop mentally more quickly than their southern or continental counterparts, and capacity to understand is of course an individual characteristic, there is a view that by the age of eight a child is clearly able to distinguish between right and wrong, to know how to act accordingly, and that, if he or she knowingly steps out of line, should be held accountable.

Intellectual assailment of this reasoning would fill volumes, but the unsophisticated experience of the Scottish police lends support. It is not unknown for a child of seven years ten months, sent out by his parents to steal in a big store, in the full knowledge that if discovered he cannot be charged, to reply cheekily when apprehended "You can't touch me I'm under age".

The case in which I came to play a central part, however, was rather more serious than the furtive and illegal acquisition of a piece of cold supermarket chicken—attempted murder.

A girl barely nine years old, living in a block of Glasgow tenement flats, had an altercation outside a flat on a level below her own home with another girl. Nothing unusual in that. Her cold, calculating anger, however, was such that she broke off the discussion stamped upstairs to her own flat and returned armed with what is an essential piece of equipment in every such Glasgow home, the breadknife. This it is said in jest, is always readily available unless father has gone to the Rangers – Celtic match and taken it with him.

The breadknife she promptly plunged sharply into the body of her young adversary.

Tut, tut. Naughty, naughty little Jemima. What was to be done with her? No nanny to scold her, no dispatch to bed in disgrace without supper and, heaven forbid in such an enlightened age, no question of the most minimal physical chastisement. An admonitory wag of the finger perhaps.

The parents of the victim not surprisingly felt less tolerantly inclined however, and the police were soon informed. The police do not prosecute in Scotland. A salutary safeguard of the citizen. They merely supply information to the Procurator-Fiscal, the Crown prosecutor in the region, who decides what steps to take. In cases of some delicacy or difficulty—as this clearly was—he refers the matter for guidance to the Crown Office in Edinburgh.

In this case Crown Counsel issued instructions which were quite clear. The wielder of the breadknife being legally accountable, and, make no mistake, having stabbed someone in a manner which might well have resulted in death, should be charged with attempted murder.

I must confess that in eleven odd years as a junior and over twelve years as a practising Queen's Counsel I had seen a lot of what was on offer, but nothing quite like this. Now after a mere nine days on the Bench, I had the task of dealing with her, having of course, no part in putting her there.

So, as Jemima appeared in the dock, pled guilty and was disposed of, wires hummed, typewriters chattered, and tongues wagged all over Scotland, England, Europe, Canada and the USA

The BBC in London awarded it second spot on the National News, accompanied by a large photograph of myself which would not have stirred the memory or the bosom of any former girlfriend. Next day some tabloid dailies outraged at the charge, burst blood vessels in their condemnation, with pride of place going to Keith Waterhouse who wailed in hysterical sympathy for Jemima "How can you mend a butterfly's broken wing?"

I noticed no similar concern for the fortunate surviving recipient of the sharp end of the breadknife or the anguish of her family. Some butterfly, some wing.

Across the Channel Paris Match joined in the chorus and devoted two full pages to "Monsieur le juge" (myself), not flattering, again accompanied by a large photograph. Mail addressed to me from Europe and America arrived by the sackful. The monster in the case, at this stage was clearly not the child but myself. Norman Wylie QC, the Lord Advocate, who was then in Canada told me later how his whole programme had been interrupted and he had been besieged by the press over there seeking an explanation for what they deemed extraordinary judicial procedure.

Back to the disposal of Jemima and my options. An absolute discharge i.e. to be sent away with a "wigging" perhaps but not a recorded conviction? No. An admonition, again perhaps with a "wigging" but no penalty? No. A deferral of sentence to await what she might do in the meantime? No. A fine? Clearly, no.

Probation? Certainly an option to be considered carefully, but in practice clearly out of the question. How could one release her to return to the same, but now violently hostile, environment to continue living beside the victim and her family with, indeed, no guarantee that the performance would not be repeated? You can well imagine the outburst of criticism which would have descended on any judge had he thus imposed probation and a further attack had followed. What a fool to let her out would have been the popular cry.

Prison for a child of eight? No. The option was not legally open but, in any event, would not have been in my contemplation. Detention? This is the point at which the dam of outrage burst.

I suppose that to the ignorant and indignant in Europe and America, both press and public, detention conjured up the vision of a little child howling in hopeless anguish as she beat her tiny hands against solid iron bars.

Being "detained" which seemed to me to be the only appropriate option in the circumstances meant no such thing. It merely meant her removal to a restricted environment for a limited period which would ensure that no member of the public would be at risk. There her development could be monitored and the medical authorities would have an opportunity to observe how her mind "ticked", and whether she was likely to be a danger to the public in future. So detention was imposed.

Inevitably there was an appeal and of course the probation report which I had ordered was available for the Appeal Court.

Well now, surprise, surprise. In the meantime other forces were at work. The Local Authority were at hand to help in a solution. This was not good publicity for poor old Glasgow. They could see, like myself, that as matters stood Jemima could hardly be released and sent back to the same environment.

Significantly however they were in a position to move the goal posts in a way not open to the Court.

They decided that Jemima and her family, who were their tenants, should be offered a better council house in a different area, far removed from the scene of the attack and their offended neighbours. "Nice work if you can get it", might have been the view of others waiting patiently on the housing lists who would have welcomed such an opportunity but who as law-abiding citizens, were given no chance to jump the queue.

The effect of this offer which was accepted with alacrity changed the whole picture dramatically.

Lord Wheatley in the Appeal Court, in a carefully worded judgement was now at one fell swoop able incidentally to assuage the public outcry by substituting probation for detention, where Jemima's behaviour could still be monitored as I had deemed necessary, but under supervision but far away from her previous home and neighbours and thus, as he thought, without the necessity of her detention.

A word about the press. Over the years I had been accustomed to dealing with them regularly in law and in sport and in politics, and had many friends amongst them to some of whom I was indebted, sadly mostly now dead. Here I had no problem with the local press, but others quite frankly behaved in a way which an independent judiciary in a free society should never have to tolerate.

Apart from appreciating the impropriety of it I wonder what intelligent member of the press would telephone to seek comment from the member of the Bench who had disposed of the case.

Others astonishingly by-passed the telephone and sought a personal approach. As I slipped quietly out of a side door of the High Court building in Saltmarket, Glasgow after passing sentence while a battery of photographers waited at the front, to walk along by the river Clyde to have lunch in the lovely old woolclipper "Carrick", formerly City of Adelaide built in 1864, which served as the R.N.V.R. Club (Scotland), an alert journalist spotted me and pursued me with all the will if not the pace of an Olympic sprinter. " Excuse me sir" he panted desperately as he caught up "I'm from the London Evening Standard. I wonder if I might have a word with you" Had I been of a different mould be might well have had two words.

He at least was more open than another reporter who sneaked on board Carrick at the forrard end via the galley and, mingling with members, stood patiently behind the group I joined in the hope of catching any utterance I might make about the case. Fruitless. Although everybody I spoke to before and during lunch knew about the case no one was tactless enough to mention it, not even, ironically, a well-known Scottish newspaper writer who was by chance amongst those present on board.

Well, some might say charitably, journalists, poor chaps, have to earn a living and may be fearful to return to their editors without a story. Nonsense. Acting within the ambit of their own sphere of activity rightly they are quite at liberty and have plenty of scope to criticise vehemently Court decisions even if, unlike as in Court those of a contrary view sadly, and against natural justice, do not get a similar opportunity to reply. But surely any attempt to harass the judiciary should be trodden on swiftly by a higher authority if there be one in the country, than the media.

While thus hurled briefly on to an international stage I can say now personally that I felt no anxiety. I did not bat an eyelid or lose a wink of sleep. I had simply done without fear or favour, and without any outside consultation, what I thought appropriate. At a higher level Lord Wheatley was generous and gave no hint of criticism. Lord Wilson of Langside, Q.C. kindly took the trouble to write to me afterwards in a highly supportive way, for which I was grateful more grateful than he himself was many years earlier when resident in a Glasgow hotel and his wife telephoned him from Edinburgh. "I'm terribly sorry" said the receptionist to her, "Mr Wilson isn't here. Would you care to speak to Mrs Wilson?" Needless to say, the receptionist had contacted another Mr Wilson.

The old crone in Edinburgh was no doubt not alone in her sentiments, but the vast bulk of mail addressed to me I imagine hostile, was never passed on by Court staff. It simply went to be shredded along with the rubbish.

Nine days on the Bench and landed with a "Nine days' wonder". Soon as always the press and the public went off to bark up a different tree, and all was peace.

To myself the frightening sequel was not the experience which I had undergone in the ordinary course of judicial duty, but the thought that emotion could be stirred over two continents and guided along a particular channel of prejudice and anger to such an extent by the media.

It gives one food for thought as to what may happen when more important issues are involved; more important even than the coverage afforded to the death of Princess Diana, and the trials of O.J. Simpson and Louise Woodward in America, to mention a few names which will readily trip off the public tongue.

I have no idea where the two little girls who fell out with each other may now be. If both are alive they will be in their thirties. I hope that Jemima has found peace with no permanent damage to the delicate membrane which held the knife, and that her victim having survived such a vicious attack from one so young has no lasting scars.

53.

BY YON BONNIE BANKS

Public Inquiries. There is always someone agitating for one, or promising one, or refusing one; and always a host of lawyers, technical experts and witnesses ready waiting in the wings to be locked away for ages in their own private little world going through the lucrative—nowadays—motions of conducting one in the language of inquiry-speak-gobbledygook.

In 1962 there were not so many long ones. No one was likely to celebrate two birthdays while taking part in one, or to make a quick fortune. The idea of going into a third year to discuss the building of an additional runway at an airport would have been considered absurd.

The Dean of the Faculty of Advocates then was anxious that important ones should be conducted by Senior counsel acting as reporters to hear and appraise the evidence and to make recommendations to the Secretary of State for Scotland. It was not just a case of getting the Faculty's oar into an important seam of work. It was genuinely felt that counsels' training equipped them better for the task than, for example, retired civil servants, and that they would find it easier to look at matters objectively. The Lord Advocate may not have been un-sympathetic to this view.

The cynical whispers, which would have been hotly denied elsewhere were that civil servants might be more disposed to "rubber stamp", an application, perhaps on the basis that it might earn them a certificate of "reliability" and thus increase the likelihood of them being invited again to preside over additional inquiries, thus providing a regular source of jam to top the bread and butter of their pensions.

In the end of the day, of course, while the reporter would issue his findings, and make his recommendations to the

Secretary of State, it had to be remembered that it was the Secretary of State who made the final decision.

In 1962 the particular inquiry which I was invited to conduct and report on involved proposals for a huge hydro-electric development by the North of Scotland Hydro-Electric Board, embracing Dalmally, Loch Sloy and an area of considerable scenic beauty and tourist attraction including Loch Lomond and Loch Katrine. It was held in the Village Hall at Aberfoyle.

Apart from the Hydro Board, the promoting authority, there were counsel representing Glasgow Corporation, Dunbartonshire County Council, Perth and Kinross County Council, Stirling County Council as well as a number of private objectors. Including inspection, as well as evidence and speeches it lasted for some twelve days. A mere minnow by modern standards, but still quite an important inquiry. The inspection found me bumping through Glengyle in a "weasel" and embarking at Stronachlachar for a sail on Loch Katrine, a welcome respite from the cramped quarters of the Village Hall at Aberfoyle.

In due course when it was all over I received a transcript of the written evidence large, bound typewritten volumes, and having read the notes began to give serious consideration to my proposed recommendations. This involved a time to read, time to think and time to formulate one's conclusions. Before completing my report, however, I received a call, a unique call.

One day my door-bell in Heriot Row rang. This was not to announce a solicitor with the customary nervous client attending for consultation. The gentleman who arrived and was ushered in was professionally dressed, a total stranger to me, and unaccompanied.

He gave his name, stated that he was a civil servant from St Andrews House and that he wished to have a word with me. Curiosity as much as anything else prompted me to offer him a seat in my consultation room. Clearly he had not come to ascertain the colour of the carpet or the wallpaper in my chambers.

He explained to me that he was from the government department who were concerned with the Inquiry which I had just conducted. This struck me as odd and rather irregular.

If I was curious and wondered what his business was, I did not take long to find out. He was clearly seeking some advance information as to what my recommendations were likely to be. I was genuinely flabbergasted. The idea that someone can approach a "judge" before he has issued his "judgement" and ask him how he is going to decide the matter was a totally alien concept in my mind. Even nowadays when I hear the word "leaks" I am naive enough to think firstly of a Welshman's garden. However, when I hear almost daily of "leaked" documents I subscribe to the view that anyone thus in breach of trust divulging confidential information should be sacked. I say this despite the recollection that in the mid-thirties much of the "ammunition" Winston Churchill fired at a slothful government in Parliament about German ambition and our military unpreparedness was said to have come from similar sources.

In order to "help" him I agreed to discuss a few questions but made it plain that I would be doing so on a purely hypothetical basis. I had not of course then decided on my findings and would not have been in a position to leak information. One hypothesis which he raised was that I should be one hundred per cent in favour of the promoting authority.

When another was mooted that I might be largely in favour of the promoting authority, but might find partially in favour of one of the private objectors, he suddenly looked askance. I was having him on, but revealing nothing.

The question for me to ask him struck me at once. Donning the mask of naiveté I enquired gently:— Is it your experience in inquiries of this nature that the promoting authority generally gets what it asks for?

He confessed, in fact that it was. Had he, I wondered, come seeking an advance unofficial confirmation that I would show him a green light? Of course.

Well I said, jokingly, you seem to have a much higher record of success than many who litigate in courts.

It was time to close the brief discussion and he departed.

What he did not know was that at one stage I had touched briefly on the actual recommendation which if not decided, as indeed it was not, but which was in my contemplation to make —roughly 4/5 success to the promoting authority and 1/5 to a private objector.

Soon I drafted my detailed report, together with my recommendations, and in time this was placed before the Secretary of State for Scotland for his consideration. It was, as I knew, competent for the Secretary of State to reject totally the findings in such a report and deal with the matter as he thought fit.

I awaited, as did every one else involved, the Secretary of State's decision.

It was published. To my enormous satisfaction, and indeed great delight, the Secretary of State accepted everything contained in my report, even down to a recommendation I made which was not usual then, that the successful private objector should be awarded his expenses. Thus it appeared that the report had been prompt, efficient and satisfactory.

On the question of money, I should perhaps add for the amusement of any present day lawyer who is involved in such inquiries that for conducting the whole inquiry and writing my voluminous report I was paid from recollection the princely sum of approximately two hundred and thirty five guineas.

I must confess that in the light of the expeditious and clearly acceptable manner in which apparently I had conducted this inquiry, I confidently expected that requests for me to conduct other important public inquiries would follow.

Not so. From that far-off day in 1962 until now, a period of thirty-six years, I have never once been asked to preside over any other public inquiry of any description large or small. Not even for the teeniest one day hearing of the siting of a new petrol-filling station.

Very, very strange.

Was I too objective in my approach? Did someone stamp my card as "unreliable"? I shall never know. Certainly the person who mattered the Secretary of State for Scotland was quite happy with me. Somewhere for some unknown reason somebody of influence was not.

A year or two ago I bumped into Sir Alan Peacock, an old university contemporary whom I had not seen for many years; professor, athletics blue, war-time naval intelligence officer and D.S.C.; you may recall that he conducted the mammoth BBC Inquiry during the Thatcher government. I recollect that the Prime Minister was not too happy about his report on the BBC A much larger fish than my little minnow.

Our brief exchange and reminiscence in a railway station did not touch on inquiries, but his parting shot delivered airily gave food for thought:— "Well, Archie, you and I are just two old rebels". His tongue, I fancy, was in his cheek.

Maybe the trouble is that a lot of influencial people do not have the capacity to realize that to be of independent mind does not make one a "rebel". It's just that I am not pompous or poker-faced or a boot-licker and take seriously the view that when acting judicially or quasi-judicially one should genuinely act without fear or favour. An old-fashioned conception?

There's nothing "unreliable" about that.

54.

FEARSOME FOURSOMES

May 1950. The tall spare figure of Bill Grant, K.C., later M.P. for Kelvingrove, Solicitor-General for Scotland and then Lord Justice-Clerk, stood scanning through thick spectacles, not a label on the bottle of whisky which bore his name, and to which I can vouch he was not averse, but the large notice-board placed temporarily above the fireplace in the Advocate's Robing Room in Parliament House, Edinburgh.

As "O.C. Golf" it was his duty to organise his troops, and to see that the annual outing on the first Monday in May to Muirfield, the home of the Honourable Company of Edinburgh Golfers, to play the first and second rounds of the Scottish Bench and Bar Foursomes went off smoothly.

Much planning was involved.

All participants from senior judges to lowly junior advocates were carefully handicapped. Firstly, they were placed in separate categories—A, B, C and D in descending order, not of rank, but of ability or inability. Then next, an A was partnered with a D and a B with a C. Each individual pairing was given its own numerical handicap, in an endeavour as it were to balance the scales of justice, and in theory to produce an even contest. Genius, said Carlyle, is an infinite capacity for taking pains. A pious hope, however, more often than not defeated by an abundance of human frailty occasionally to be measured in gin, or kummel, or both.

There were further complications.

The exigencies of legal practice were wont to compel sudden withdrawals, even at the eleventh hour, and replacements had to be found quickly for those who had to settle instead for the disagreeable task of going to work. Delicate balance at this stage played no part. The body of any advocate would suffice.

Little did I know, while waiting for the bell to call my case in Court, that Bill was in predatory mood, and intent on bagging a quick "victim"— a late substitute for a defecting, and no doubt defective, golfer.

Being the only person at hand he explained his predicament to me with his usual disarming and genial smile. Then suddenly pointing a finger he said benevolently, more as an instruction than a request, "You'll play".

My response seemed adequate. "I'm sorry, but I don't play golf".

"That doesn't matter" he replied arily, dismissing my plea as irrelevant.

"But I don't have any clubs" I retorted desperately; a total waste of time.

"We'll find you some" he assured me dismissively as he walked out. It was all fixed.

Of course as a child I had been on a golf course—but without a lesson, without a clue, and with little enthusiasm. The idea of any game where one didn't try to run like the wind or engage in sharp physical contact seemed to me then to be designed solely for geriatrics. However, I consoled myself with the recollection that although I had once won a fountain pen in a schoolboy putting competition, this would not infringe my amateur status. It was also curious to reflect that while at St Andrews University although I had represented the University at rugby football, association football, hockey and cricket, I had never even once struck a golf ball on any of the St Andrews courses. Time was to change that.

Now, however, had come the time to pay the penalty for youthful arrogance.

Clubs were duly provided and, equally important, a partner. He of course was an A (handicap 3) R.A. (Bob) Inglis whom I knew well even before we went to the Bar, later Sheriff at Dundee, Fort William and Paisley. I was of course a D—for duffer (handicap my technique and a strange set of tools).

Muirfield (or "Myawfield" as some of its Parliament House detractors were wont to mimic) was skilfully planned so that matches might start conveniently at the first or tenth hole. I was aware that the course consisted of eighteen holes since the chosen number has neither been dictated by dozens or decimals but has its historical origin in the fortuitous lay-out at St Andrews, "the home of golf", the number finally fixed in 1764.

To the tenth and to the test.

The flight path of our ball bore no resemblance to that of the crow. There were several abortive take-off's and several forced landings, but eventually we reached the green. It was a close run thing. We lost the hole in a ten to an eleven. This loss, however, was not all gain to the enemy. I detected a weakness in my D opponent, Ewan Stewart. To my untutored eye his swing seemed better designed for the swift decapitation of chickens on a conveyor belt than the smooth propulsion of a golf ball. So it proved.

We won.

The nineteenth hole I approached with a confidence born of experience and, being pleasantly re-invigorated my partner and I waited to discover our second round opponents.

A fine Tory–Socialist alliance. G.E.O. Walker K.C. from Newark Castle—not the one where King John is buried and J.G. Leechman, later Lord Leechman. Curious to think that it was the latter's fiercely socialist uncle who is alleged to have declared passionately during the unrest on Clydeside after the First World War that they would hang the judges from the lamp-posts.

As our match progressed, however, his nephew a kind and

mild mannered fellow, might easily have formed similar homicidal tendencies toward his Etonian partner who found post-prandial golf all too difficult.

Again, we won.

There was now a delay of some six weeks before the third round. Fired with success, and flushed with enthusiasm for this new sporting activity, I began to indulge in solitary clandestine visits to the Braid Hills. There for sixpence a round ($2^{1}/_{2}$p) one could practice on a public course to one's heart's content. I was secretly elated with my progress. When the third round arrived I was no longer a genuine D. A C? perhaps even a B? The "enemy" were in for a shock.

Again, we won.

The next round? Again we won.

So eventually, Bob (who was vastly amused) and I stood on a late July afternoon on the first tee of the delightful Bruntsfield Links Golfing Society course ready to play in the final of the Bench and Bar Foursomes. It seemed a long time since May.

Our opponents were formidable. J.M. Cowan later Q.C. and a Sheriff in Glasgow, partnered by C.H. Johnson, later a Q.C., Sheriff in Glasgow and Sheriff-Principal of South Strathclyde. Only Cowan, however, was formidable in a golfing sense— handicap 1 and playing on his home course. He struck the ball beautifully but, alas, his partner was not scratch or up to scratch, showing a distinct preference for sand rather than grass, and on one occasion for fresh air.

After seven holes we were seven up.

"Keep going" said my partner with a grin as Johnston discovered another bunker, "I've never won a golf match 10 and 8".

We won by 7 and 6 (the final)

These were highly significant figures in the law. At that time

7/6 was the annual price of a dog licence. 7/6 was also the weekly sum awarded in aliment to the mother of an illegitimate child such as my client, a cinema usherette who was said to have conceived in the back row of the stalls. I cannot recall the name of the film but it may be that she was not in a position to tell me.

Golf however, I had now decided was a wonderful game, and assuredly for young athletic people as well as geriatrics.

So by 1951 I was a member of Bruntsfield for the princely sum of £25 entry money and £8.8/- subscription and, having duly submitted score cards, presented with my first golf handicap—12. In 1955, a few days sadly after I had resigned, I was approached to join the Council there. Instead in 1956 I had the good fortune to be elected a member of the Royal and Ancient Golf Club of St Andrews; £20 entry money and £12 subscription. Arthur Sievewright, the eminence gris of St Andrews handicapping, like a sinister figure from Conan Doyle, tracked me secretly one day, garbed in his heavy cape, and I was given a handicap of 8. No chance of winning anything with that.

But golf and the law were now irrevocably intertwined. The All Spheres Club (a golf club confined to fifty people in Parliament House) held a number of competitions so that I now possess a replica of the Morison-Montgomery Quaich for winning the original (gifted by Sir Ronald Morison Q.C., the father of the present Lord Morison and George Montgomery, Professor of Scots Law in Edinburgh University) My victory was rendered more probable when they ignored my disclosure that I was 8 at St Andrews and insisted in starting me off with 18 in the All Spheres Club.

Golf and the law were also entwined internationally.

For some there was the chance to play at Muirfield or Woking against the English Bench and Bar led by the

redoubtable Sir Godfrey Russell-Vick Q.C. whose son Clive
was a close friend of mine and in the same form at school. For
others there were matches at Royal Portrush and Muirfield
against the Northern Ireland Bench and Bar. The anecdotes
are too numerous to recount.

Those from Dublin, who were not yet in on the act,
declared that there was a great future at the Northern Ireland
Bar - for anyone who could read and write. At Portrush we
drank from the Curtis Cup and were cheered by the presence
of the silvery haired nonagenarian Sir Anthony Babington who
had been Attorney General during "the troubles". At Muirfield
on buying a whisky for an opponent Billy Doyle I was told by
his partner that to Billy "it was just like posting a letter". Sure
enough he tossed it into the horizontal gap in his face where it
disappeared in one. Poor Billy. Later he came out of his Roman
Catholic Church one Sunday morning to be shot dead on the
spot by the IRA   Lord McDermott, another opponent, who
had been Lord Chief Justice in Northern Ireland and also sat
in the House of Lords told me that the two best counsel who
appeared in the Lords in his time were "Morison and
Shawcross". Interesting.

It is a long time since May 1950. As I sit in the Big Room
in the R. and A. and watch the world's best golfers I have a cosy
fellow feeling. I too have been a winner.

The real warmth I feel, however, is for Bill Grant, in days
of depression the only person to be called to the Scottish Bar
in 1934. When we stood for neighbouring Parliamentary
constituencies in Glasgow (1955), he for Kelvingrove which
had recently filched my best area - and I for Maryhill, he spared
considerable time in his own home, in kindly fashion, to give
the benefit of his experience to a political "rabbit".

We do not know where our destiny leads us, but I wonder
what would have happened if he had not on that day in May
1950, said "You'll play".

55.

A BREATHLESS HUSH

When the public think of lawyers I suppose that they more readily associate flannel with their tongues than their trousers, and silly point with their arguments rather than a position on the cricket field.

It was June 1955. The splendid pre-war cricket match between the Army "Garrison", in Edinburgh and the Faculty of Advocates, a casualty of changing society had long since lapsed, but now many a moth was to be disturbed as eager advocates reached inside their wardrobes to discover whether their old flannels could still accommodate their older waistlines.

I had arranged with two solicitors, each with a fair cricket pedigree and the intelligence to instruct me professionally, W.F.M. Whitelaw (Grange) and W.R. Courtney (then captain of Carlton) to raise a side from the Bar to play Parliament House (solicitors, apprentices and clerks) whose eleven, over the years, boasted a number of club cricketers solicitors such as Gordon Hay (Edinburgh Academicals) Herbert Macpherson (Murrayfield) George Henry (Royal High School F.P.) and P.G.H. Younie (Carlton) the last good enough I would say as an ex Scottish selector to have played for Scotland.

The response was enthusiastic and soon was recruited not only an experienced eleven but an umpire and scorer as well. The volunteer umpire G.E.O. Walker Q.C., of whom you already know, impressed and astonished everyone by wearing an M.C.C. tie. Whether he had ever been to Lord's was not clear but he explained that someone had put him up for membership after the First War when M.C.C. were short of cash—for £200. Those now on a twenty year waiting list to join must be vastly amused.

The scorer, James Fiddes, later Q.C. and Sheriff at Hamilton, was a Baliol man, a classicist who thus found no difficulty in dealing with the word 'extra'. The spectators, mainly Bar wives and girl-friends, sipped their gins as they giggled nervously at the antics of their heroes. Despite some sterling performances we lost, but no matter the match was a great success, and obviously to be repeated.

Next year, Lord Wheatley, a keen sportsman, who as a young soccer player he assured me over a glass of orange juice (his, not mine), had taken all the penalty kicks over five years for Shettleston Juniors and never missed one, anxious not to be condemned to a life sentence on the boundary, approached me and asked, "Archie, would you like to make it Bench and Bar?" A splendid suggestion, which from 1956 onwards became a permanent feature.

The influx of the judiciary raised our morale if not our playing strength. Yet in 1956 we won a famous victory: famous because by the time I finally left the Bar in 1973 it was the only victory which I can recollect and a rare occasion for me to take 6 wickets for 73 and make 34 not out.

The real pleasure, however, was not to be found in cold statistics but in the human and humorous incidents involving many legal celebrities which might have surprised the public, who would only have associated them with formal and solemn occasion   Lawyers are not all stuffy and detached from life, (some are).

So now to indulge the luxury from random reminiscence of pulling back the curtain—or should it be the sightscreen—at different matches and revealing, without murmuring of judges, a few comments on some. The rank given them was not necessarily held at the material time.

"Emslie and Kincraig came forth to bat. As usual they opened with care". I have of course substituted their names for the

Lancastrians, Hallows and Makepeace, in that classic piece in which Neville Cardus began the description of his wedding day.

Lord Emslie, Lord President and Lord Justice General was, over the years, the most successful batsman. He accumulated runs consistently in sober-like rather than Sobers-like fashion with the care of his judgements and the tenacity of a Boycott, but I would never have thought it necessary to post a fielder for him on the long-on boundary unless it were to sign autographs a precaution which I would have deemed unnecessary. He was also a fair slip fielder.

Lord Kincraig an avid disciple of relevancy in court and also a useful wicket keeper, batted with a compact confidence playing neatly off his legs, but driving towards mid-wicket less forcibly than Peter May.

Lord Robertson a stout guardian of New Club and Muirfield membership and again a useful wicket keeper, and bat for Grange as well as at Oxford, brought a relaxed and imperious attitude to the crease. When bowled all ends up, ignoring the death rattle behind him, he calmly threw the ball back to the bowler and said "Have another shot". The umpire did not intervene, the startled bowler duly obliged, and he continued to enjoy (for a brief spell) the luxury of a second innings.

Lord Guest a Dean of Faculty who had not yet gone to the House of Lord's was more circumspect. He proceeded elegantly to the crease wearing my brand new Old Leysian sweater to which as a Merchistonian he was not strictly entitled. Some idiot promptly bowled him a straight one and having been "Merchiston Castled" he returned to the Pavilion amongst sympathetic murmurs rather than to the applause which greeted Don Bradman in his last Test when, needing only four to have a Test Match average of 100, he returned with a similar score.

Lord Wheatley was seen to both advantage and disadvantage.

To advantage when a damaged leg compelled him to make use of a "runner". The runner astutely chosen and sportingly agreed by the opposition, was none other than Menzies Cambell now Q.C., M.P., an international sprinter who had recently captained the British Athletic team and played rugby on the wing in the final of the Middlesex Sevens. To disadvantage on another occasion when facing the last over at 0 not out he failed to appreciate that runs were irrelevant and if he had just held on, the match could be drawn. We watched anxiously and counted while his Lordship parried the first five balls of the over without getting off the mark. Unfortunately in a rush of Celtic blood, having decided that he would alert the scorer he struck the sixth ball a short distance, less far than the swashbuckling and sartorially conscious Lord Grieve would have done, and set off to run without the aid of Menzies Campbell.

Realising immediately as a fielder swooped that he had made a hideous mistake he turned to go back. Alas in doing so he fell flat on his face, was run out, and we lost the match off the last ball.

The murmurs in the pavilion were less sympathetic than those accorded to Lord Guest. It was suggested that whatever his judicial competence he was not the best judge of a run. His son Sheriff John Wheatley, now in Perth, did better for Grange. I sat with father on the day he scored his only century there.

Over the years many more legal personalities on both sides at different times dotted the outfield. On the Parliament House side one could not fail to notice solicitor W.G. Moodie W.S. who was one of the larger dots or Campbell Walker W.S., an Oxford rugby blue, who fed me leg-breaks as sweet as chocolate profiteroles which sat up outside the off-stump waiting to be scoffed. Of those who reached the Bench by having a safe pair of hands (judges are meant to have safe hands) it could not be said that they all brought the same hands to the cricket field.

Lord Dunpark, my patient and charming devil master did, it is true, one season catch mumps.

Lord Leechman, Lord Mayfield a good wartime M.C., Lord Cowie (a Scottish rugby internationalist), Lord McCluskey and Lord Kirkwood all spread themselves about the ground at different times. Sheriff Neil Gow, when not instructing solicitors to instruct him, also fiddled in the outfield Sheriff Dick Scott did not set the field alight, having left his pipe in the dressing room while Menzies Campbell ran like a Liberal Democrat.

Sheriff-Principal Jock Mowat was only concerned with a cricket ball dropping from the sky and not as later with an aircraft which fell to earth in Lockerbie, a catch which he fielded excellently in terms of his report.

Choosing a bowler, I always found, was a problem, but the sibilant Lord Cameron ("bouffant" not father "Jock") and Lord Sutherland were wont to take a turn with the ball while onlookers were merely more likely just to take a turn. Sutherland was less accurate but more dangerous than Cameron, but I speak relatively. Like Mike Proctor, the brilliant South African, he bowled "off the wrong foot", but less predictably. I recollect one ball where, had there been goalposts instead of stumps, the keeper might have watched it pass without bouncing over the bar before the umpire signalled four byes.

It can of course be said in his defence that tactically it is always a good idea to keep the batsman guessing. The element of surprise should not however, be extended to everyone else on the field or, for that matter, in the ground. It is, however, to his credit that as others in the judiciary wilted he still took the field when aged fifty-six to preserve the side as 'Bench and Bar'.

All those I mention have now returned to the Pavilion and

some sadly have been given 'Out' by the Great Umpire in the sky. There were no camcorders to record them for posterity and even the scorebook which I nursed carefully for many years —surely a potential collector's piece—disappeared when passed into other hands: clearly not into a safe pair of hands.

In a world where public relations are of paramount importance, and sadly self-projection, as I have indicated elsewhere, may be a greater factor sometimes than real ability in personal advancement, it would have been no bad thing if the public's perception of the law in action had been given a truer perspective by an opportunity to hire from the video shop a film of the Bench and Bar v Parliament House cricket match.